THE BANG
AND THE
WHIMPER

THE BANG AND THE WHIMPER

Apocalypse and Entropy in American Literature

ZBIGNIEW LEWICKI

CONTRIBUTIONS IN AMERICAN STUDIES,
NUMBER 71

GREENWOOD PRESS
WESTPORT, CONNECTICUT
LONDON, ENGLAND

Library of Congress Cataloging in Publication Data

Lewicki, Zbigniew.
    The bang and the whimper.

    (Contributions in American studies, ISSN 0084-9227 ;
no. 71)
    Bibliography: p.
    Includes index.
    1. American fiction—History and criticism.
2. Apocalyptic literature—History and criticism.
3. Entropy in literature. I. Title. II. Series.
PS374.A65L4 1984   813'.009'353   83-12678
ISBN 0-313-23674-7 (lib. bdg.)

Library of Congress Catalog Card Number: 83-12678
ISBN: 0-313-23674-7
ISSN: 0084-9227

First published in 1984

Greenwood Press
A division of Congressional Information Service, Inc.
88 Post Road West
Westport, Connecticut 06881

Printed in the United States of America

10 9 8 7 6 5 4 3 2 1

Copyright Acknowledgments

Quotations from *Invisible Man* by Ralph Ellison,
copyright © 1952 by Ralph Ellison, are reprinted
with the permission of Random House, Inc.

Quotations from *The Origin of the Brunists* by
Robert Coover are reprinted with the permission
of Robert Coover.

Some say the world will end in fire,
Some say in ice.

Robert Frost, "Fire and Ice"

CONTENTS

ACKNOWLEDGMENTS

This book was written between August 1980 and August 1981, when I was a Fellow at the Woodrow Wilson International Center for Scholars in Washington, D.C. It is a truly unique institution which provides a most stimulating forum for the exchange of opinions among scholars from many fields. We have all profited from these exchanges, and while I have expressed my special gratitude to some of my colleagues in person, I am indebted to everybody who spent that year at the Center. Like all Fellows, I was impressed with the good will and expertise of the permanent staff; their willingness to accommodate our requests made life so much easier.

I am also grateful to the staff of the Huntington Library in San Marino, California, where some parts of this book were drafted in the summer of 1979. The peaceful atmosphere of the Library and its unique holdings made working there a pleasure.

My friends and colleagues read various parts of the manuscript and offered most valuable comments. I would particularly like to thank Thomas Blues from the University of Kentucky and James McClintock from Michigan State University, as well as Milton Reigelman from Center College, Kentucky, for their insightful suggestions. The book was finished as planned only because Deborah Van Buren, my research assistant, helped me with her extraordinary diligence.

INTRODUCTION

Sweeping statements about national literatures are usually as misleading as sweeping statements about nationalities—and just as tempting. Is it not our experience that in "well-written" English novels the heroes find support in strong social structures? Does Russian literature not favor individuals who are frustrated by the inadequacies of their society and torn between a sense of loyalty and the dark dreams of their souls? Is it not true that in Polish literature the motif of patriotic duty and responsibility overshadows everything else? Are we not justified in the conviction that American literary characters mistrust their society, and consequently feel lost in it? And does this alienation not come from the sense of impending catastrophe and the fear of universal annihilation?

There are many kinds of death, and their significance varies considerably. In Polish literary tradition, for instance, one dies for *the cause*. If the death occurs during a war, one finds the ultimate reason for dying in the identification with *patria*. In American literature, on the other hand, war is considered to be a structure in which individuals define their own identity. To die means to waste this experience. If they perish, their death is a personal tragedy, not a loss for the national cause. But death can also have another dimension, which involves whole nations, or even civilizations. Individuals have no control over such destruction, and their own death is of no consequence. If it is to have any significance at all, it must be related to some higher order and explained in transcendental terms. It is this vision of total annihilation that characterizes

American literature more than any other single image. And yet American society is based on the concept of a new beginning, rather than destruction. The American Dream has changed over the years, but it continues to function and to express the concept of the Promised Land. There is no better metaphor to express this duality of fear and hope than that of apocalypse: while we do not always remember it, the true meaning of the term includes not only destruction, but also a rebirth into a new and infinitely better world.

The present study is concerned with the significance of the apocalyptic dream, its influence on the development of American fiction, processes that have led to gradual changes in its meaning, and literary devices used to express the concept of universal destruction. Chapter 1 outlines the Puritans' concept of apocalypse and its impact upon early American literature. Probably the most important aspect of seventeenth-century apocalyptic considerations was a growing sense of disappointment and unbelief that the colonists were able to fulfill their role in God's design. This feeling of a failed mission was also the reason for the increasing skepticism about America's prospects for becoming the site of the New World. While calamities continued to be interpreted as signs of God's anger, and the precarious existence of the early colonies would not permit the fear of destruction to disappear, the faith in ultimate regeneration began to erode. The short-lived fervor of the Great Awakening did not promise well for the eighteenth century either. Despite efforts to the contrary, American society was increasingly subjected to the process of secularization, and one of its effects was the loss of conviction that Americans were destined to perform the role of the chosen people.

While Michael Wigglesworth's *The Day of Doom* and Joseph Morgan's *The History of the Kingdom of Basaruah* are included in this study as evidence of dilemmas and anxieties that haunted the colonists, the late eighteenth century or even the early nineteenth century is a more appropriate time to begin an inquiry into American literature, and particularly into American fiction. Some critics believe that even this earliest phase is characterized by a preoccupation with the apocalyptic theme: George Snell, for instance, discusses Charles Brockden Brown as an "apocalyptic."[1] While such claims seem exaggerated (and Brown will not be included in the present study), one can certainly argue that the concept of apocalypse had no trouble finding its way into American fiction. It was, however, considerably changed in the process. For the seventeenth- and eighteenth-century preachers, apocalypse signified a real event. They constructed their visions around what they believed to be the inescapable fate of the world. When the idea entered literature, it became a metaphor, a conventional set of images that were used to describe nothing more than the end of the world of one novel. While similarities between such fictional worlds and our "real" universe can be drawn, there is a fundamental difference between the fear of impending total destruction and a literary description of an imaginary cataclysm. Moreover, when John Cotton preached about the apocalypse, and when Jonathan Edwards discussed it in *An Humble Attempt*, there was no doubt in the minds of their audience as to what philosophical system constituted the frame of reference for such deliberations. A similar clarity cannot be expected from literary works, which may reflect on philosophical questions, but rarely address them directly. One of the consequences of this is that the concept of *apocalyptic fiction* has never been precisely defined.

It is possible that no unequivocal definition can ever be formulated. It is in the nature of symbolic representation to escape direct description, and the best we can expect is an approximation based on the most distinctive and frequent features. In the case of apocalyptic literature it may be useful to enumerate the most conspicuous symbols of the Book of Revelation. A succession of "apocalyptic moments," suggested by R.W.B. Lewis, is perhaps the best such account. He distinguishes ten phases of the apocalyptic process:

(1) periodic natural disturbances, earthquakes and the like; (2) the advent and the turbulent reign of the Antichrist or the false Christ or false prophet (sometimes called the period of the Great Tribulation); (3) the second coming of Christ and (4) the resultant cosmic warfare (Armageddon) that brings in (5) the millennium—that is, from the Latin, the period of one thousand years, the epoch of the Messianic Kingdom upon earth; thereafter, (6) the gradual degeneration of human and physical nature, the last and worst apostasy (or falling away from God), featured by (7) the second and briefer "loosening of Satan"; (8) an ultimate catastrophe, the end of the world by fire; (9) the Last Judgement; and (10) the appearance of the new heaven and earth.[2]

If these are indeed the main apocalyptic "moments," and there seems to be little quarrel with Lewis' assumptions, then apocalyptic fiction perhaps can be best identified by the presence and intensity of related images. Ideally, a novel would include situations that can be traced back to all these elements of the apocalyptic vision. However, this is very rarely the case. It is therefore important to establish which of these images must be present in a work of fiction if it is to be classified as apocalyptic literature. It seems that the indispensable elements are the Antichrist figure, the battle between the forces of light and the powers of darkness, and the destruction of the book's world by violent means. The last element is particularly crucial, and no other image can be substituted for it.

On the other hand, rebirth, or the appearance of the new heaven and earth, is the core of the religious apocalypse, but is not always present in works of fiction. Its absence indicates a fundamental change that occurred when the concept of apocalypse was adopted by secular literature, where it was increasingly understood to denote destruction rather than rebirth. John R. May calls this the "secular" apocalypse, as opposed to the religious one,[3] but the problem seems to be deeper than such a juxtaposition would indicate. While the increasing secularization of American life was indeed the main cause for the reduced role of the concept of rebirth in the apocalyptic structure, there were also other reasons. The new waves of non-Protestant immigrants, the influence of expanding capitalism, the political events of the period, including the devastating Civil War—these were only the most conspicuous among the varied, and frequently conflicting, factors that were shaping American consciousness in the nineteenth century. The ensuing confusion has been documented by social historians, as well as by historians of literature, and the change in the meaning of apocalypse is an indicator of the direction of more fundamental changes in the American mind.

The two writers chosen in order to study the changing concept of apocalypse in nineteenth-century American literature are Herman Melville and Mark Twain. There is little doubt that *Moby Dick* is the most important nineteenth-century American novel, and no analysis of the period can be complete without it. But there is also another reason for including *Moby Dick*. The book is generally considered to present a pessimistic view of the world, and the final destruction of the *Pequod* is interpreted as support for such an opinion. Yet it is contended here that Melville followed the traditional apocalyptic pattern, in which the universe is destroyed only to be reborn. The survival of Ishmael is more than a literary device: after all, the story could have been told by a third-person narrator. Melville may not have been certain about the shape of the new world, and the novel ends with Ishmael emerging from the vortex; but his reappearance constitutes a clear indication of the rebirth that will follow. On the other hand, it is symptomatic that the confused nineteenth century virtually rejected Melville because of the alleged pessimism of his works: the history of Melville's reception reveals as much about American society as the history of Shakespeare's reception tells us about the changing cultural criteria of the modern world.

The other nineteenth-century American writer included in the study is Mark Twain. Unlike Melville, he was interested more in social phenomena than in philosophical concepts, yet toward the end of his literary career he attempted to combine questions about society with broader problems concerning the ultimate destiny of our world. *A Connecticut Yankee in King Arthur's Court* and the *Mysterious Stranger* manuscripts are perhaps the best literary manifestations of the uncertainties and anxieties of the American fin-de-siècle. The concept of rebirth is a religious one, as it assumes some form of posthumous existence. It could not, therefore, be reconciled with the scientific fascinations of the period. Yet the waste resulting from irrevocable death, individual or universal, was inconsistent not only with Puritan values, but also with scientific principles, and Mark Twain's dilemmas were shared by many of his contemporaries.

The fear of waste was intensified by the discovery of the law of entropy. The essence of the theory is that the universe is subordinated to a constant and irreversible process of "dying" or, more precisely, of turning its energy into waste. The process can be neither stopped nor reversed—and there will be no regeneration. It is contended here that the concept, if not the term, was first used in American literature by Herman Melville in *Bartleby the Scrivener*. The reason why the entropic imagery of the story has gone unnoticed for so long may be that no other writer followed Melville's lead. While the term was made more popular by Henry Adams at the turn of the century, American literature of that time, and of the next fifty years, was not receptive to either entropic or apocalyptic visions.

Insofar as they can be compared at all, the concept of apocalypse and the concept of entropy contradict each other in almost every respect. One is physical, the other metaphysical; one is based on moral distinctions, the other on indifferent scientific laws; one promises violent destruction and regeneration, the other slow but irreversible decay; one leaves room for hope, the other does not. Yet by describing the end of the world both concepts transcend our experience and go beyond our reality. If they are to become literary themes, they must be expressed through symbolic structures, and the dominance of the realistic-naturalistic tradition in American literature made this virtually impossible.

Consequently, apocalypse and entropy virtually disappeared from American fiction of the first half of our century, with the possible exception of Nathanael West, who did not, however, win recognition in his lifetime. While some critics consider William Faulkner an apocalyptic writer,[4] his works do not seem to fall into this category. Apocalypse must be discussed as a religious structure. The nature of a particular god may vary, but a man-made disaster, even if it is "final," should not be called apocalyptic, or the term loses its relevance. Faulkner's world is not deprived of God, but its processes are almost invariably secular. Even the journey with Addie's body in *As I Lay Dying* is not a religious undertaking but a proof of man's ability to prevail in the most hostile circumstances. The destruction of the South and its values is caused by men, by their greed and ruthlessness—not by God.

Both apocalypse and entropy were revived as literary concepts in the 1950s and 1960s, and all major contemporary writers have dealt with these ideas. Ralph Ellison used apocalyptic imagery to express the conflict between white and black cultures, which in *Invisible Man* are shown as two worlds that not only are different now, but will remain separate forever. Robert Coover's books provide evidence that postmodern literature can imitate apocalyptic structures, but that it is too self-referential to express concepts rooted in the tradition of moral judgement.

The concept of entropy is at least as popular, particularly because it can be applied to several aspects of contemporary life. Thomas Pynchon is best known for providing a literary equivalent for physical entropy, and William Gaddis has created in *JR* a picture of a world that has fallen prey to informational entropy. Yet the metaphor of entropy is broader than its roots in physics and cybernetics would suggest, and novels by Susan Sontag and John Updike are also analyzed in an attempt to combine the concept with the concern for moral values that has traditionally dominated American fiction.

With the exception of the seventeenth-century writings, this study deals exclusively with fiction, and is concerned only with works that provide new insights into apocalyptic and entropic imagery. It does not deal with other literary genres or with quantitative problems of the relative popularity of these concepts in the course of American literature. Its main aim is to follow the development of apocalyptic and entropic tendencies in American literature in order to explain the fascination of American writers with the vision of universal destruction. While such imagery is intrinsic to the whole tradition of American Puritanism, it is also inseparable from the American fascination with science. The religious element, however, stresses hope, and the scientific attitude is concentrated on the inevitability of destruction. The interaction between the two and the relative dominance of one over the other in American fiction have been significant indicators of the changes in the American consciousness.

NOTES

1. George Snell, *The Shapers of American Fiction*, pp. 32-45.
2. R.W.B. Lewis, *Trials of the Word*, pp. 196-97.
3. John R. May, *Toward a New Earth*.
4. Cf. ibid., pp. 92-114; Richard Pearce, " 'Pylon,' 'Awake and Sing!' and the Apocalyptic Imagination of the 30's," pp. 131-41.

THE BANG
AND THE
WHIMPER

1

THE APOCALYPTIC TRADITION

As Mircea Eliade convincingly demonstrates,[1] the concept of the cosmic cataclysm resulting in the destruction of the world appears in virtually all systems of religious belief. It is presented almost invariably as a repeatable event which happened in the past and will occur again in the future. When Judaeo-Christianity incorporated the idea, it introduced an essential innovation that was a consequence of its concept of linear and irreversible time (as opposed to a cyclic mode of existence, assumed by most religions). Unlike its equivalents in other religious systems, the Judaeo-Christian end of the world can occur only once. When the world is destroyed, it will reappear as a purified New World, where there is no evil. Regardless of whether the End of the World will be announced by the coming of the Messiah, or by the second coming of Christ and the Last Judgement, it is a basically optimistic image that the faithful should welcome rather than fear. At the same time, the events that precede the end can, and should, convey the sense of God's anger. The believers will suffer through a period of terror and persecution, and the forces of evil will temporarily increase. This combination of hard times and hope for a blissful future accounts for the fact that many persecuted Christian sects perceived their fate as a sign of an approaching millennium: earthly sufferings were a small price to pay for eternal happiness. The arrival of the Reformation, together with the ensuing persecution of various religious groups, added considerably to the popularity of millenarian beliefs. One such group was the English

Puritans. They were forced to leave their country in order to escape persecution, and most of them settled in America.

While the concept of the apocalypse was one of the predominant ideas of the New World, its origins go back to the Old World. In his *Millennium and Utopia*, Ernest Lee Tuveson shows how sixteenth-century European Protestantism followed the earlier tradition of "pessimistic apocalypse," according to which the millenarian decline had already begun. Early in the seventeenth century, however, Joseph Mede, a great Biblical scholar, reinvigorated the concepts formulated by the early Christians, who had claimed that the Millennium was yet to come and would bring about a period of happiness for mankind. According to Tuveson, Mede's commentaries gave "the apocalyptic movement an entirely new direction, which was to make it ultimately the guarantor of secular and religious progress alike, rather than the harbinger of decay and a pessimistic prospect for mankind."[2] Consequently, when the first colonists left for America they took with them a basically optimistic view of the apocalypse, even if the Puritans' convictions differed from those of the English Protestants, and even if the most prominent of the former were soon to dispute Mede's interpretation.

The arrival of the Puritans in America was a direct result of their escape from persecution. In less immmediate terms, however, they perceived their coming as a promise that they would participate in God's design to create the New World. This sense of mission and its consequences have been discussed at length by the scholars of the period. Probably the best illustration of the colonists' zeal and their willingness to bend reality to their millenarian hopes is provided by their persistent attempts to convert the American Indians to Christianity. The colonists were aware that the apocalypse was to be preceded by the conversion of the Jews: the arrival of the New World was dependent upon the completion of the process. In order to reconcile their hopes with reality, some theologians offered "proofs" that Indians were descendants of a lost tribe of Israel.[3] Even those who, like Richard Mather, were not convinced by such theories frequently believed that if Indians could be taken away from Satan, so could the Jews.[4] Perhaps the most concise expression of the special role assigned by the colonists to the Indians can be found in John Cotton's sermon to the passengers of the *Arbella*, which he concluded by reminding the colonists that they should

offend not the poore Natives, but as you partake in their land, so make them partake of your precious faith: as you reape their temporalls, so feede them

with your spirituals: winne them to the love of Christ, for whom Christ died.
They never yet refused the Gospell, and therefore more hope they will now
receive it. Who knoweth whether God have reared this whole Plantation for
such an end.[5]

It was also John Cotton who constantly reminded the colonists about
the apocalyptic ramifications of their mission. Having settled in Mas-
sachusetts, he embarked upon a long series of sermons devoted to the
exposition of various passages from the Book of Revelation. Only some
of the sermons have survived, but there is plenty of evidence provided
by his contemporaries to establish the influence of Cotton's preaching
upon the apocalyptic inclinations of clergy and laymen from all over
the colony.

In one of the sermons, based on the fifth chapter of the Book of
Revelation (*and power was given him to continue forty and two moneth*),
Cotton calculated the date of the fulfillment of the apocalyptic prophecy.
Having surveyed possible meanings of the "forty and two moneth" of
the Beast's power, he concluded that the phrase could only stand for
"1260 days," as it would be inappropriate to speak directly of "days"
when referring to the powers of the night, and it "is a Propheticall
phrase in mysticall Scriptures" that "a day" means "a year." Consequently the power given to the Beast—which, in Cotton's interpretation, is the Roman Catholic church—is thus to last for 1,260 years.
Cotton then searched for a possible beginning of this period, and accepted two possibilities: the year 300, the time of Emperor Constantine;
and the year 395, when the Pope was first called Pontifex Maximus.
Cotton's conclusion was that the power of the Beast had ended in 1560
(the Pope's Bull against Elizabeth) and would end again in 1655, which
presumably would also mark the beginning of the Millennium. While
aware of his own limitations, Cotton seemed to have little doubt as to
the accuracy of his reasoning:

I will not be two [*sic*] confident, because I am not a Prophet, not the Son of a
Prophet to foretell things to come, but so far as God helps by Scripture light,
about the time 1655. there will be then such a blow given to this beast, and
to the head of this beast, which is *Pontifex maximus*, as we shall see a further
gradual accomplishment and fulfilling of this Prophesy here.[6]

The world did not end in 1655, nor on any of the dates offered by
other prophecies. Nevertheless, the widespread interest in the apoca-

lypse was not shattered, largely because "Apocalypse can be disconfirmed without being discredited [which] is part of its extraordinary resilience."[7] However, while the Puritans preserved their faith in the apocalyptic design, they also realized that they had to earn their place in it, and it was not long before the preachers began to scold their congregations for failing to observe the moral standards they had set for themselves. Doubts appeared as to whether the Puritans deserved the role of the chosen people, but the apocalyptic dreams were not easily abandoned: "Even while invoking the specter of national covenant, the ministers retain the dream and amplify its meaning; as fact and ideal veer further apart, they restructure experience in terms of . . . the realm of the imagination."[8]

This duality of hope and castigation, incitement and despair, became the chief feature of the American jeremiad, as well as of such literary forms as narratives, histories, diaries, and poems. One such early chronicle of New England is Edward Johnson's *Wonder-Working Providence*, completed in 1651. For the purposes of the historian, Johnson's book is an unreliable source; it is usually scorned by students of American Puritanism as biased and naive. When considered as a literary text, however, *Wonder-Working Providence* can provide us with a new perspective on the Puritans' mission in America. Johnson's visions differ from those of John Cotton or the Mathers, but at the same time he comes closer to expressing the views of the less sophisticated, average colonist.

For Johnson, America is to be the field of the battle between Christ and Satan, and he is convinced that the colonists will play a special role in the events to come. He also has no doubt that the Millennium has already begun and that the true meaning of the settlers' errand into the wilderness is that they will participate in the process of renewal and purification:

> Thou hast thy prime and middle age here spent,
> The best is not too good for him that gave it,
> When thou did'st first this Wilderness frequent,
> For Sions sake it was, that Christ might save it.[9]

Johnson believes that Antichrist has already established control over some parts of the world, and that the faithful should help Christ bring his opponent's power to an end. To achieve this, living a simple and virtuous life is not enough, and Johnson advocates an active path of fiery fight. Only such determination can result in a total victory and prevent Antichrist from gaining more ground. Accordingly, Johnson keeps referring to the true believers in military terms, such as "Souldiers of Christ, as they are shipped for his service in the Western World" (p. 24); only after the final victory "shall the time be of breaking Speares into Mattocks and Swordes into Scithes."

While Johnson is convinced that the Millennium has already begun, he also believes that it will be a long time before its aims are completed: "These are but the beginnings of Christs glorious Reformation, and Restauration of his Churches to a more glorious splendor than ever" (p. 23). But Babylon has fallen already, and the followers of the Roman Catholic church have fallen with it. Those who still have doubts should overcome them, or face the consequences of their hesitation: "Behold his swiftness all you that have said, where is the promise of his comming?" (p. 24). Christ is coming "on that white Horse" to fulfill the prophecy of the Scripture—and it is the American colonists who will fight for his cause and who will subsequently be rewarded when the New World arises on the rubble of the old one.

Johnson also addresses himself to the problem of the literal, as opposed to the symbolic, understanding of the apocalypse, which "some suppose . . . onely to be mysticall, and not literall at all: assuredly the spirituall fight is chiefly to be attended, and the other not neglected, having a neer [sic] dependancy one upon the other" (p. 232). While he frequently "elevates his material in a manner that tends toward the allegorical,"[10] he does not shun straight didacticism. Perhaps the most direct parallel between the Biblical prophecies of the apocalypse and the contemporary state of events comes when Johnson talks about "proud Bishops . . . the heathen Romans your predecessors, after they had banished John to the Isle of Pathmos, suffered him quietly to injoy [sic] the Revelation of Jesus Christ there: here is a people that have betaken themselves to a newfound World" (p. 104*).

"It hath been the longing expectation of many, to see that notable and wonderfull worke of the Lord Christ, in casting down that man of sin who hath held the whole world . . . under his Lordly power" (p. 230), says Johnson in what is clearly an expression of the hopes of the early colonists. They left civilization and chose the wilderness so that they could participate in God's work. Their faith in the purposefulness of His design was complete. They firmly believed that the destruction would be followed by regeneration and that they would enter the New World. But if apocalypse remained an optimistic concept, it was also a terrifying one, and the combination of these two aspects of the End is best exemplified by Michael Wigglesworth's poem, *The Day of Doom*, which also marks the first time that apocalyptic ideas were expressed in America in an unmistakably literary text.

The Day of Doom was published in 1662, and immediately became the first American best seller. It is estimated that a copy of the book "was sold for one out of every twenty persons in New England."[11] There were at least seven editions before the end of the seventeenth century, and many more in the eighteenth century, and even though the poem was subsequently reduced to the state of a literary relic, its impact upon the New Englanders cannot be overestimated.

The Day of Doom seems to us a cruel work. Contrary to what might be expected, however, its original readers were not frightened: according to Perry Miller, even the children loved it.[12] The reason for such a reaction can be found in Wigglesworth's belief, expressed in the poem, that those who are prepared for the End have nothing to worry about. Needless to say, all of Wigglesworth's readers considered themselves righteous, and therefore did not feel threatened by the poem's descriptions. They hoped that they did not have to fear the Day of Judgement, even if it came unannounced—which is exactly what happens in *The Day of Doom*. Such suddenness was obviously meant to increase the sense of terror:

> So at the last, whilst men sleep fast
>   in their security,
> Surpris'd they are in such a snare
>   As cometh suddenly.[13]

Christ appears, while "the Earth is rent and torn," and his coming causes terror and panic:

> The wild Beasts flee into the sea,
>   so soon as he draws near, . . .

Amazeth Nature, and every Creature,
  doth more than terrify.

(XV, 7-8; XIV, 7-8)

The Judgement itself is carried out in the same mood. The saints are granted eternal bliss, but when various types of sinners begin to approach the Judge's throne, they encounter what can best be described as vengeance. In an interesting twist of logic, Wigglesworth even suggests that the saints will derive pleasure from witnessing the sinners' punishment and their pain; that such *Schadenfreude* could be reconciled with sainthood was one of the peculiar features of Puritanism:

The Saints behold with courage bold
  and thankful wonderment,
To see all those that were their foes
  thus sent to punishment.

(CCXIX, 1-4)

Wigglesworth must have perceived the obvious questions that would be raised by portraying not only the saints, but also God, as merciless and cruel, for he had the sinners ask:

"How can it be that God should see
  his Creatures' endless pain,
Or hear their groans and rueful moans,
  and still his wrath retain? . . .
"Can God delight in such a sight
  as sinners' misery? . . .
Oh thou that dost thy Glory most
  in pard'ning sin display, . . .

(CXXXI, 1-4; CXXXII, 1-2, 5-6)

But God's only explanation is that his patience has been exhausted:

"It's now high time that ev'ry Crime
  be brought to punishment;
Wrath long contain'd and oft restrain'd,
  at last must have a vent.
Justice severe cannot forbear
  to plague sin any longer,

> But must inflict with hand most strict
>   mischief upon the wronger.
>
> (CXXXIX)

Obviously enough, when writing these lines Wigglesworth had in mind not so much the Judgement Day as his own times. The colonists sinned, and if the image of the chosen people was to survive, fundamental changes had to be brought about. It seemed to some that the best solution was to frighten the misguided souls into a virtuous life. But Wigglesworth's God is cruel even when he is unlikely to have such a purpose in mind, and nowhere is it more clear than in the famous passage dealing with condemned children who are sent to hell for what is clearly Adam's sin, not theirs:

> "Not we, but he ate of the Tree,
>   whose fruit was interdicted;
> Yet on us all of his sad Fall
>   the punishment's inflicted.
>
> (CLXVIII, 1-4)

But God rejects their plea and does not grant them salvation. This scene has drawn considerable attention from readers and critics, even though Wigglesworth's attitude did not really differ from that of most Puritan theologians. What is, however, more significant is that Wigglesworth's alleged "cruelty" is an internal contradiction in his poem. Replying to other sinners' pleas, Christ says:

> "God did ordain sinners to pain,
>   yet he to Hell sends none
> But such as swerv'd and have deserv'd
>   destruction as their own.
> His pleasure is, that none from Bliss
>   and endless happiness
> Be barr'd, but such as wrong'd him much,
>   by willful wickedness.
>
> (CL)

The children obviously do not fall into this category, so why are they punished? It seems that the answer can be found outside the poem, in a major theological development that occurred in the same year that

Wigglesworth's poem was published: the adoption of the Halfway Covenant. The issues of original sin and baptism, or admission to the church, were not identical. They were, however, similar enough to draw the conclusion that if those "who dy'd in infancy" and "from the womb unto the tomb were straightforwardly carried" were guilty and did not deserve the Savior's grace, there was indeed very little ground to argue that the children of Puritan saints were blessed merely because their progenitors were among members of the church. Seen in this light, *The Day of Doom* was a book that addressed itself to one of the most disputed theological problems of the day.

If Wiggleworth's condemnation of infants can be interpreted in the light of contemporary events, it also has to be placed in a broader context. The concept of the Judgement Day was a topical one for Wigglesworth's readers, and they perceived his description of it as an impending reality rather than as a fantasy outside time. From this perspective, *The Day of Doom* possesses all the characteristic features of traditional apocalyptic literature. It presents a very gloomy and frightening picture of the end of the world, but at the same time it offers a hope that "devastation would be a preliminary to regeneration." Wigglesworth's readers had no doubt that they were a part of this process and that America was the place where God's work would begin, a belief strengthened by the poet's vision that the earth itself was not doomed to destruction. Whatever Wigglesworth's limitations as poet or prophet, his vision was shared by his contemporaries, who believed that rebirth was an indispensable part of the apocalypse.

In the period that followed (the last quarter of the seventeenth century), interest in the apocalypse increased even further. The reasons were twofold. On the one hand, the year 1675 marked the outburst of King Philip's War, which threatened the New Englanders and suddenly made real the possibility of total destruction. The warfare began on June 20, 1675, and while Philip himself was killed in August 1676, the hostilities continued, with varied intensity, until a peace treaty was negotiated and accepted on April 12, 1678. While the numbers of people involved on both sides were not large at first (Plymouth, for instance, was requested to contribute 158 men to the forces of the New England Confederation), the war lasted long enough to account for the death of every sixteenth New Englander of military age. Moreover, it was a war for survival, and the colonists feared not only for their own lives, but also for the future of their New World. Unity and better organization finally tipped the scale in their favor, but the sense of having their physical existence threatened remained with them for a long time. Their mood can be discerned not only from the titles of theological discourses, such as *The Times of Man Are in the Hand of God*, but also from the newly instituted ceremony of covenant-renewal, which was to reaffirm the special place occupied by the colonists in God's design.

The other reason for the increased interest in the apocalypse was connected with the heightened sense of the colonists' failure to fulfill the role of the chosen people. Such fears were never far away, and had been voiced almost since the creation of the first colonies. They were expressed with particular intensity in 1679 in the document of the Boston Synod, written by Increase Mather, titled *The Necessity of Reformation*.

The text has been analyzed and discussed by numerous students of American Puritanism, both for its description of the New Englander's manners and for its evaluation of the mind of the colonists. The picture painted by Mather, and approved unanimously by the representatives of the churches, is almost uniformly grim. The colonists are found guilty of behaving irreverently, wearing inappropriate apparel, Sabbath breaking, abuse of alcohol, idolatry, and displaying inordinate passions. They are also said to lack public spirit, break promises, neglect family, abuse the name of God, disregard church fellowship, and display too much pride; some are even guilty of opposing the work of reformation. All these sins, some more serious than others, are used by Mather to convey his main message, which is his apprehension about the colonists' ability to fulfill their role in God's design to create the New World.

The Necessity of Reformation begins with the reminder that "it was a great and high undertaking of our Fathers, when they ventured themselves and their little ones upon the rude waves of the vast Ocean, that so they might follow the Lord into this Land."[14] God punishes the colonists for their sins with "a mortal Contagion," "devouring Fires," and "fearfull Desolations in the Earth," but lest some people think these plagues are too harsh a punishment, they have to remember that "our iniquityes admit of sadder aggravations than can be said of others, because we sin against greater light, and means, and mercies then [*sic*] ever People (all circumstances considered) have done; and therefore the Lord is righteous in all the evil that hath befallen us" (p. iv). With all the punishments meted out by God so far, the colonists have not yet seen the most severe one. If they do not improve, God may very well deprive them of their status as the chosen people and leave them out of His apocalyptic scheme:

It is a solemn thought, that the Jewish Church had (as the Churches in New-England have this day) an opportunity to Reform (if they would) in Josiah's time, but because they had no heart unto it, the Lord quickly removed them out of his sight. What God out of his Soveraignty may doe for us, no man can say, but according to his wonted dispensations, we are a perishing People, if now we *Reform* not. (p. v)

While the document of the Boston Synod accurately expresses the anxieties of the colonists, their hope for the New World, and fears about their own place in the apocalyptic events, it is not a work of literature and cannot be analyzed as such. In fact, most works of this period should be classified as "writing" rather than as "literature." The main reason is, of course, the Puritans' condemnation of works of fiction for "their tendency to excite and foment impure flames." We must also remember that practical professions were of much greater importance for the early colonists than the ability to create literature. While works like Cotton Mather's *Magnalia Christi Americana* include numerous stories not much different from those of Washington Irving or James Fenimore Cooper, the imaginative minds of the times concentrated on religious texts. Sermons were frequently beautifully planned, carefully composed, and skillfully delivered: they could in fact be considered works of sacred art.

At the same time, one should not forget the warning of Perry Miller, who concluded his study of the early Puritans' style by saying that

any criticism which endeavors to discuss Puritan writings as part of literary history, which seeks to estimate them from any "aesthetic" point of view, is approaching the materials in a spirit they were never intended to accommodate.... We shall do nothing but misread the literature if we do not always remember how their great teacher, William Ames, had told the Puritans, "That key is to be chosen which doth open best, although it be of wood, if there be not a golden key of the same efficacy."[15]

The problem becomes even more acute with Jonathan Edwards. Most of his writings, and particularly "Notes on the Apocalypse," cannot be considered literary texts. At the same time, no discussion of the apocalyptic tradition in American culture can be complete without considering Edwards, "the greatest artist of the apocalypse in America." His views on the apocalypse are important not only because "American literature begins ... with the narratives, sermons, diaries .... of the New England Puritans" and because "some of the prominent themes in later works ... first become articulate with the colonists,"[16] but primarily because Edwards' doubts, contradictions, and hopes are the real key to the period: "Can one indeed begin to comprehend the eighteenth century, with its ultimate revolutions, unless he recognizes the apocalyptic spirit in which it was conceived?"[17]

Edwards' treatment of the apocalypse epitomizes the fascinations, as well as the contradictions, of eighteenth-century America. He was the country's foremost theologian, prepared numerous commentaries on the Bible, and devoted significantly more time to the Revelation of St. John than to any other book of the Bible. He was well aware of the discoveries of Newton, Halley, and other ground-breaking scientists of the immediate past, and fully understood that his interpretative work differed from theirs; yet, with all his disclaimers, he formulated his speculations concerning the place and time of the End as if they constituted irrefutable scientific evidence. Edwards' knowledge of European rational philosophers was unmatched in America, but this did not prevent him from displaying chiliastic inclinations that bewildered even his admirers. He went as far as to prophecy the date of the End, a mistake that cost him an inordinate measure of criticism and embarrassment. He also kept secret "Notes on the Apocalypse," which were not published until 1977.

The "Notes" are a series of interpretations of specific chapters and verses of the Book of Revelation. For the most part, these explanations constitute another attempt at unravelling the mystery of St. John's vision and relating it to the known history and geography of our world. In one of the most interesting fragments, Edwards, following not only John Cotton, but many other theologians as well, tries to establish the actual duration of the Beast's reign over the earth (Rev. 13:5). As the general understanding was that the forty-two months, referred to by St. John, actually mean 1,260 years, the main question was to establish the date when the period began. According to Edwards, "The forty-two months began in the year 606, when the pope was first seated in his chair, and was made universal bishop. They will, therefore, end about 1866."[18] Edwards thus does not expect the End to happen very soon, particularly since he also considers it possible "that Satan's kingdom in the world will not be totally overthrown, his ruin will not receive its finishing stroke till the year two thousand'' (AW, p. 129). He is equally cautious about establishing the actual location of the kingdom of God, and believes that ''the land of Canaan is the most advantageously posited of any spot of ground on the face [of the earth], to be the place from whence the truth should shine forth, and true religion spread around into all parts of the world'' (AW, p. 133; brackets in the original). While ''the Mediterranean Sea . . . opens the way from Canaan directly to America,'' and thus enables the miraculous work to reach the new continent expeditiously, Edwards does not argue at this point that it is America which will first witness the work of God.

It was not long, however, before topical events caused Edwards to change his mind. The initial success of the Great Awakening made him proclaim that ''we can't reasonably think otherwise, than that the beginning of this great work of God must be near. And there are many things that make it probable that this work will begin in America.''[19] He then proceeds to establish ''evidence'' that such is indeed the Lord's design.

First, God's work was to begin on ''far off isles,'' and Edwards ''can't think that anything else can be here intended but America'' because the isles ''are spoken of as at a great distance from that part of the world where the church had till then been.'' He further argues that ''providence observes a kind of equal distribution of things.'' Asia witnessed the beginning of God's work; Europe was the site of many glorious events, but also ''shed the blood of the saints and martyrs of Jesus.'' So it is only just that ''God has . . . reserved the honor of building the glorious temple to the daughter, that has not shed so much blood.'' The historical events also seem to bear this concept out: '' 'Tis worthy to be noted that America was discovered about the time of the Reformation, or but little before: which Reformation was the first thing that God did towards the glorious renovation of the world'' (GA, pp. 355-356).

Edwards' final argument is that ''the first shall be last, and the last first'':

When God is about to turn the earth into a paradise, he don't begin his work where there is some good growth already, but in a wilderness, where nothing grows, . . . 'tis probable that he will begin in this utmost, meanest, youngest and weakest part of [the earth]. (GA, p. 356)

Not only did Edwards change his mind about the location of the New World, but he also thought that the commencement of God's work was not so far away: "And if these things are so, it gives us more abundant reasons to hope that *what is now seen in America*, and especially in New England, may prove the dawn of that glorious day" (GA, p. 358).

Edwards soon came to regret these prophecies, and ultimately felt victimized by "slanderous" reports about his alleged claims that "the millennium was already begun, and that it began in Northampton."[20] While Edwards himself did distinguish between the belief that the Great Awakening announced the beginning of God's work, and an assumption, which he never made, that the revivals actually signified the beginning of the process, the distinction could have been easily overlooked, or even maliciously misinterpreted, by others. Moreover, at the conclusion of *An Humble Attempt* Edwards proposes an "extraordinary united prayer" that should begin in November 1746, and continue for seven years (AW, p. 435). Again, he does not say that the completion of this period will at the same time mark the beginning of God's work, but he does create an image which, given the general inclinations of his audience, could easily be interpreted as setting forth a chiliastic prophecy.

While Edwards was probably the most influential theologian of his times, similar ideas can be found in the writings of other preachers of the early eighteenth century. This is also the first time that apocalyptic ideas can be traced in a work of literary fiction: in an obscure book by Joseph Morgan. "If *Pilgrim's Progress* is to be reckoned as one of the early examples of the English novel, then *The History of the Kingdom of Basaruah* may well be called the first American novel," according to Richard Schlatter.[21] Originally published in 1715, *The History* could perhaps have been considered one of the antecedents of the American novel if the genre itself had developed in the New World in a manner commensurable with its rise in England. Unfortunately for Morgan it did not, and his book passed into oblivion. When mentioned at all, *The History* is generally included among utopian literature—and thus "mistreated" again. Its basic structure is not a fictional description of an imaginary land, aimed at providing an ideal solution to mankind's problems, but a religious allegory based on man's progress from the Beginning to the Last Judgement. It also provides literary evidence of the presence of apocalyptic ideas in the cultural consciousness of early America, though *The History* is not a book about the apocalypse. Unlike in *The Day of Doom*, the millennial considerations occupy only a small part of the text, which is also devoid of the pyrotechnical effects so lavishly displayed by Wigglesworth.

What makes *The History* an important element of the apocalyptic tradition is not its description of "that part of the land of *Basaruah* which lies toward the North of America"[22]—which is simply another confirmation of the widespread belief concerning the location of the New World—but Morgan's treatment of the Last Judgement. *The History* differs from *The Day of Doom* in its acquiescence to the excessive fears raised by the Calvinistic vision of the merciless apocalypse. While Wigglesworth had supported the premillennial concept in which the end of the world would descend upon unprepared people, Morgan believed that the Last Judgement would be preceded by a period of a thousand years when people would be given a chance to repent for their sins. The number of the saved could thus increase considerably: "Before the Great General Court, there was a Period of Time called *Ta Chilia Ete*, wherein the Prince was Resolved to shew all the World his Power and Conquest over the Rebellious *Ruhoths*" (p. 155).[23] Most people could thus earn salvation even if their past lives would not have warranted it: "It is thought that there went as many or more People over the River of *Regeneration* during the *Chilia Ete*, then [*sic*] all that went to the *Sulpherous Pit* before that time" (pp. 156-157).

Salvation was offered to all those who demonstrated an honest effort to earn it, and even though some failed to avail themselves of the opportunity, many were saved. On the surface, then, Morgan's view contradicts Wigglesworth's. What makes them part of the same tradition is that *The History* is preoccupied with people's inability to observe covenants and earn salvation. The millennial hope appears, somewhat artificially, toward the very end of the book, and is not very convincing. It may be assumed that Morgan was inclined to follow the traditional Calvinistic approach, according to which the number of the Elect was very small, and the Preterites deserved their fate by being unable to make use of God's good will. At the same time, Morgan's views must have been altered by his conviction that such a vision of the millennium was no longer popular and that people would need to be offered more hope if they were to remain in the church.

Morgan's *History*, published in a period of changing religious attitudes, never generated the power and influence of Wigglesworth's apocalyptic work. The exact nature of these changes is not easy to determine, although Alan Heimert, H. Richard Niebuhr, and—in a different way—

LeRoy Edwin Froom have added considerably to our understanding of the period.[24] For a literary critic, however, the eighteenth century is not very fertile ground. The great historical changes of the times were not accompanied by important developments in fiction, and the poetry of the period was of little consequence. Only the last two decades of the century brought about a major change, and the arrival of writers like Charles Brockden Brown, Washington Irving, and James Fenimore Cooper signalled the emergence of an independent American literature of the nineteenth century.

Apocalyptic ideas and imagery abound in nineteenth-century fiction. Writers and readers of the period were familiar with the Puritan tradition. Its vitality is proved by such works as Nathaniel Hawthorne's *The Scarlet Letter*, which recreates Puritan customs and value systems. A broad interest in the apocalyptic theme constitutes further evidence that the nineteenth century accommodated some fundamental concepts of earlier times. James Fenimore Cooper's *The Crater*, Edgar Allan Poe's "The Fall of the House of Usher," and Nathaniel Hawthorne's stories are examples of diversified literary realizations of apocalyptic ideas. These concerns found their most powerful expression in the works of Herman Melville, especially in *Moby Dick*, which was neglected for more than half a century after its publication. *Moby Dick* opens itself to a variety of critical interpretations. Placed in the apocalyptic tradition, the novel indicates that the concept of the end of the world continued to permeate the American mind despite fundamental changes in the role that religion played in the everyday life of the country.

NOTES

1. Mircea Eliade, *Myth and Reality*.
2. Ernest Lee Tuveson, *Millennium and Utopia*, p. 76.
3. Cf. Allen H. Godbey, *The Lost Tribes: A Myth*; J. F. Maclear, "New England and the Fifth Monarchy," pp. 243-46; Sacvan Bercovitch, *The American Jeremiad*, pp. 77-80.
4. See also Richard Mather's discussion of John Eliot's contention that "our *Indians* are the posterity of the dispersed and rejected *Israelites*, concerning whom our God has promised, that they shall yet be saved by the deliverer coming to turn away ungodliness from them." *Magnalia Christi Americana*, p. 560.
5. John Cotton, *Gods Promise to His Plantation*, pp. 19-20.

6. John Cotton, *An Exposition upon the Thirteenth Chapter of the Revelation*, p. 93.

7. Frank Kermode, *The Sense of an Ending*, p. 8.

8. Sacvan Bercovitch, "Horologicals to Chronometricals," p. 6.

9. Edward Johnson, *Wonder-Working Providence of Sions Saviour in New England*, p. 169. Subsequent references in parentheses are to this edition.

10. Sacvan Bercovitch, "The Historiography of Johnson's *Wonder-Working Providence*," pp. 141-42.

11. Kenneth B. Murdock, Introduction to Michael Wigglesworth, *The Day of Doom*, p. iii.

12. Perry Miller, *Errand into the Wilderness*, p. 218.

13. Michael Wigglesworth, *The Day of Doom*, stanza IV, lines 5-8. Subsequent references in parentheses are to this edition.

14. Increase Mather, *The Necessity of Reformation*, p. iii. Subsequent references in parentheses are to this edition.

15. Perry Miller, *The New England Mind: The Seventeenth Century*, p. 362.

16. A. W. Plumstead, "Puritanism and Nineteenth Century American Literature," p. 222.

17. Perry Miller, *The New England Mind: From Colony to Province*, p. 188.

18. Jonathan Edwards, *Apocalyptic Writings*, p. 129. Subsequent references in parentheses, preceded by AW, are to this edition.

19. Jonathan Edwards, *The Great Awakening*, p. 353. Subsequent references in parentheses, preceded by GA, are to this edition.

20. Stephen J. Stein, Editor's Introduction to Edwards, *Apocalyptic Writings*, p. 29.

21. Richard Schlatter, Introduction to Joseph Morgan, *The History of the Kingdom of Basaruah*, p. 3.

22. Joseph Morgan, *Kingdom of Basaruah*, p. 33. Subsequent references in parentheses are to this edition.

23. *Ta Chilia Ete* = thousand years; *Ruhoths* = spirits.

24. Alan Heimert, *Religion and the American Mind*; H. Richard Niebuhr, *The Kingdom of God in America*; LeRoy Edwin Froom, *The Prophetic Faith of Our Fathers: The Historical Development of Prophetic Interpretations*.

2

MOBY DICK: APOCALYPSE AS REGENERATION

Herman Melville's *Moby Dick* is without question one of the most important American novels of the nineteenth century, yet its greatness went unrecognized for dozens of years. Numerous explanations have been offered, such as the discrepancy between the complex mythical structure of Melville's novel and the relative unsophistication of his audience. While those factors cannot be underestimated, it is possible to suggest a different, and perhaps more important, reason—a rejection of the misunderstood apocalyptic message of Melville's epic.

When *Moby Dick* was published in 1851, the United States seemed to be fast approaching the peak of its power. In 1848 the treaty of Guadalupe Hidalgo ended the Mexican War and confirmed the acquisition of Arizona, California, Nevada, New Mexico, and Utah, as well as parts of Colorado and Wyoming. Three years before, Texas had been annexed. A series of treaties settled the Canadian boundary, while the Clayton-Bulwer Treaty of 1850 was understood to put an end to British influence in Central America and secured American rights in the future canal that would link the Atlantic and Pacific oceans. With the Civil War still a decade away, and the sense of power effectively muting most social questions, the United States seemed to be on its way to power and glory.

At the same time, however, we must not forget that, despite the generally optimistic mood of mid-nineteenth-century America, the times were not always reassuring. Revolutionary movements shook Europe during the late 1840s, and new immigrants transferred some disquieting ideas to America. The fear of a possible catastrophe was increased by the Great Famine, which decimated Ireland. When the Irish arrived in the United States they brought with them tales of horror and a real sense of an ending. Such millennial concepts were received in America with compassion: the American Bible Society, the American Tract Society, and the American Home Missionary Society, as well as various Sunday school societies that had been formed a few decades earlier, were now operating across the nation, contributing significantly to what is referred to as the Great Revival of the nineteenth century. William Miller's first sermon was delivered in 1831, and 1843-1844 witnessed the unparalleled growth of the Millerite movement. This combination of the optimistic course of "great" politics with visibly disquieting potential developments could not but influence, and confuse, the writers of the period.

The success of Melville's early works could be caused largely by the general acceptance of illusory happiness rather than disquieting truth, by the fact that the American and British reading public "preferred theories of natural innocence to those of original sin."[1] Melville's problem, however, was that he could not, and would not, bend his vision to fit the taste of the public. The failure of *Mardi* was a warning that went unheeded, and in 1851 Melville published *Moby Dick*, which brought him fame, but not until a century later. In his own times the book was practically rejected by the same readers who had so enthusiastically received *Typee* and *Omoo*. If, as is generally assumed, *Moby Dick* failed because of its "blackness ten times black," because of its gloom, pessimism, and pervasive mood of tragedy, it failed for all the wrong reasons. The mid-nineteenth-century public was already unable to recognize and appreciate the optimistic quality of an apocalyptic structure.[2] While many readers perceived *Moby Dick* as an apocalyptic narrative, its overall pattern of the traditional, or optimistic, apocalypse was virtually ignored.

"Call me Ishmael," the opening sentence of the narrative proper, serves Melville's purposes as no other could. Nothing and nobody exists until named, and if *Moby Dick* is to be its own self-enclosed world of words, naming (rather than creating) must be the first step. But why "Call me Ishmael" rather than "My name is Ishmael"? And why do we learn so little about him in the course of the book? While the story of the Biblical Ishmael does begin with "thou shalt call his name

Ishmael" (Gen. 16:11), it is told in full. There is, however, another figure in the Bible about whom little more than his name is known, who provides a first-person narrative, and whose identity is revealed in the first sentence of this narrative—St. John the Divine. Melville strengthens the sense of Ishmael's relation to St. John by further similarities (for instance, John's revelation came to him by way of prophecy or dream, and much is made in *Moby Dick*'s opening chapters of Ishmael's search for a place to sleep), but the essential parallel is that both John and Ishmael commence their narratives in worlds their audiences know, and go on to create visions independent of those worlds. To do this, John resorts to a very complex symbolic structure in which the symbols no longer relate to the reality we all know, but become self-referential and can be comprehended only in their own terms. Limited by the conventions of secular fiction, Ishmael cannot do the same, but has to utilize a time-honored metaphor for creating an independent and self-enclosed world within the world: a sea journey. A ship is a microcosm, and what happens there must not be judged by terrestrial criteria.

What brings *Moby Dick* even closer, not only to the Bible in general, but specifically to the Book of Revelation, is that the *Pequod*'s journey begins on December 25: Christ's second arrival on earth can only announce the Day of Judgement. This, in turn, can be understood to signify that Ahab is a Christ figure. Such interpretations have been offered,[3] and they can be substantiated not only by the *Pequod*'s sailing date, but also by some quotations from *Moby Dick* which describe Ahab as bearing ''a crucifiction in his face,'' wearing the Crown of Lombardy, and waking up ''with his own bloody nails in his palms.'' Moreover, Ahab possesses at least one important feature of the Savior: he sets out to free the world of evil, for which he pays with his own life.

And yet Ahab cannot be interpreted as a Christ figure. What makes him different from and unacceptable as Christ is his concept of evil. In his view evil, personified by the white whale, endeavors to destroy the world, and the only way to prevent Moby Dick from doing so is to annihilate it first. What Ahab fails to understand is that violence, if countered by more violence, not only will not disappear, but is bound to increase regardless of who wins the battle. Ahab does not possess the Christian sense of redemption, be it the individual sacrifice of Christ, the collective mission of the chosen people, or the ultimate chance offered just prior to the Last Judgement. Instead, Ahab seeks revenge, which only perpetuates evil. If evil is indeed Manichean and actively seeks to control the world, Ahab's violence adds to its power; if it is Augustinian and is therefore a form of the absence of good, Ahab's lack of compassion and his sacrifice of other people's lives strengthen evil even more.

Ahab is thus fundamentally different from the Savior: in the apocalyptic structure of *Moby Dick* his role is to provide an alternative to Christ's sacrifice. R.W.B. Lewis suggests such an interpretation when he says that "Ahab is the Antichrist, misleading mankind to the point of bringing down upon it the annihilating wrath of God,"[4] but this, again, is what Ahab is not. He is not the Biblical Antichrist, whose relatively simple aim is to lead as many people as he can away from God, just as Christ's clearly defined mission is to save these souls. Ahab is a more tragic figure who sets out to destroy the source of all evil and ends up adding to its power. He perishes without understanding (or perhaps refusing to understand) that his intentions turned against him and led to the destruction of his world and its inhabitants. Ahab is not "misleading mankind" the way Satan or Antichrist would. His motives are sincere and he pays the highest price for his mistake. He does not mean to bring eternal doom upon souls, yet this is what happens, his own fate being no different. Ahab goes down entangled in a harpoon's rope—a death strongly symbolic of his entanglement in irreconcilable contradictions.

Ahab is not a false prophet who leads his willing followers. Instead, he sets a goal for himself and forces others to serve him: the *Pequod*'s crew is not allowed to decide whether they want to pursue Moby Dick. There is only one exception: Starbuck, who displays free will when he resolves not to kill Ahab. His temptation, however, results not from his personal feelings about Ahab—even though the latter had earlier threatened to kill the First Mate—but from the conviction that Ahab will become "the wilful murderer of thirty men and more, if this ship come to any deadly harm; and come to deadly harm, my soul swears this ship will, if Ahab have his way.'"[5] When Starbuck puts the musket away, his decision directly contradicts Ahab's. He acknowledges his own limitations as a human being, but his refusal to take any action results in the loss of more than thirty lives. Ahab's grand plan, on the other hand, calls for the destruction of what he thinks is the cause of all evil—at almost any cost, and certainly regardless of whether the pursuit will result in his own damnation. Consequently, he emerges as an accomplished human being, whose "Ego non baptizo te in nomine patris, sed in nomine diaboli!'' (p. 421) is not so much a request for Satan's assistance as a declaration of his own independence from God's will. He is ready both to chart the course and to bear the consequences. Therefore he cannot be interpreted as Antichrist, whose main task would be to lure people away from the real faith, while he himself is placed in a position fundamentally different than theirs. Despite his role as a leader, Ahab's fate is determined by the same factors that determine his crew's fate, and the success of the challenge is equally vital to him.

If, then, Ahab is neither Christ nor Antichrist, who is he in the apocalyptic structure of the book? The answer can only be that he is Man, both great and lost at the same time. He is great because he tries, and while he cannot fulfill the role of the Redeemer, the greatness of a human being lies in not giving up; he is lost because he is unable to penetrate the intricate pattern around him. He lets himself be misguided by appearances and ends by being punished for his excessive pride; but he perishes as Adam, or as Prometheus, as someone brave enough to follow his conviction rather than conform to imposed laws. He will not repent and therefore must perish, and his example is supposed to discourage prospective followers. But Ahab has tried to hold his own in the complex, impenetrable, and godly apocalypse, and by doing so he has asserted man's duty to seek consciously his place in God's great design.

By fulfilling his obligation Ahab confirms man's active role in sacred history. He provides an optimistic version of the apocalyptic sequence, even if he himself is defeated. Ahab goes down and so do all of his crew—except for Ishmael, who survives. Ishmael's role in the apocalyptic structure of *Moby Dick* is to confirm the difference between those who will be punished and those who will be rewarded. Before the *Pequod* sailed, Ishmael had attended Father Mapple's sermon, based, fittingly, on the Book of Jonah. The story of Jonah, apart from its obvious whale symbolism, also includes an important apocalyptic comment. When the sea calms as a result of Jonah being thrown overboard, the message is clear: the innocent will not be punished for the sins of the guilty. When the *Pequod* is destroyed, Ishmael, who never quite shared Ahab's sinful passion, survives. The world will be destroyed, but the virtuous will begin a new life in the New World.

By their very nature, apocalyptic events cannot be described except through prophecy: if mankind perishes, nobody can survive to tell the story. Melville alters this tradition by introducing a narrator who not only describes the events, but does so from the perspective of historical time. The time structure of *Moby Dick* is not, however, immediately recognizable, nor is Ishmael's special status; some of his comments, prompted by events known to him but not yet to his audience, suggest that he is prophesying. The prophetic aspect of *Moby Dick* is strengthened by the fact that other characters also try to foretell the future—and Ahab is among the most conspicuous of the "seers." His prophecies are, however, of a special kind: he "foretells" desirable events in order to make them happen. At one point he says: "The prophecy was that I should be dismembered; and—Aye! I lost this leg. I now prophesy that I will dismember my dismemberer" (pp. 144-45). He did not, however, have his way, and he knew the reason very well. Later in the book Ahab seems to defy God by pretending he can control lightnings and magnetic phenomena, but regardless of what he tells his superstitious and awed crew, he is aware that playing games with Nature is not the same as successfully challenging God. Ahab vacillates between his dreams and reality, accepting signs that are favorable, rejecting those that are not, and bending facts to meet his expectations. His efforts are best summed up by "wise" Stubb, who concludes that "come what will, one comfort's always left—that unfailing comfort is, it's all predestinated" (p. 146). Ahab's greatness is created and maintained by his courage in standing up against such circumstances, but win he certainly cannot.

Ahab's failure would suggest a pessimistic interpretation of *Moby Dick*'s apocalyptic structure if it were not, again, for Ishmael. After the *Pequod* sinks into the Pacific, Ishmael undergoes a ritual death passage. He is overwhelmed and pulled down by the whirlpool, but subsequently emerges from darkness not only to tell the story of how the old world perished, but also to start a new one. The book's last word, which describes Ishmael as an "orphan," stresses the break with the past, and his prospective role as an initiator rather than a continuator. It is Ishmael's fate, therefore, that determines the optimistic aspect of *Moby Dick*'s apocalyptic message, and in order to accentuate his significance even further, Melville frequently contrasts him with Ahab.

Amid numerous and usually self-explanatory apocalyptic signs and symbols, of which Gabriel and his "seventh vial" are but the most conspicuous (and which are discussed at length in *Melville's Use of the Bible*),[6] the meaning of the Ahab-Ishmael relation for *Moby Dick*'s apocalyptic structure can easily be overlooked, yet it is essential for understanding Melville's concept of salvation. Ahab is a great man, but he is also a great sinner, and as such he will not be saved. He will suffer with most of the crew, including innocent children (Pip) and those who were not baptized (Queequeq). Although at first Ishmael does not seem to be among the elect, his behavior gradually convinces us that he is. He befriends Queequeq but refuses to participate in the savage's pagan ceremonies; goes to church before sailing; keeps his distance from Ahab; and favors Stubb and Starbuck, who at least try to challenge their iconoclastic captain. Ultimately, Ishmael is rewarded with salvation, which also completes the apocalyptic structure.

The contradictory, yet mutually complementary, character of the Ahab-Ishmael relation is paralleled by Melville's treatment of whiteness in *Moby Dick*. The equivocal quality of this color was not lost on Melville, who turned it into the central symbol of the novel. White can be associated with love and life, as well as with death and burial; these diverse meanings come together in the ceremonies of marriage (where white stands for death to the old life and the beginning of the new) and death (where white symbolizes birth into a new life). The white bridal veil signifies innocence, but the whiteness of billows is usually associated with rage. White is also the principal color of the Book of Revelation, where it appears up to eighteen times (depending on the translation), while black and green are mentioned only twice, and other colors once or not at all. In almost all of these cases, white describes clothes (garments, robe, linen) or an aspect of the physical appearance (white head and hair), but the color's symbolic function is never forgotten: some translations substitute ''white'' in several instances with ''bright'' or ''pure.'' At the same time, due to the frequency with which it appears in the Revelation of St. John, whiteness itself becomes a symbolic notion, which is further stressed by its being associated with the throne. White is thus the color of the Book of Revelation, and our understanding of its symbolism determines to a large extent the pessimistic or optimistic interpretation of the apocalypse.

The Book of Revelation abounds in mysterious and ambiguous symbols, but what makes whiteness perhaps the most confusing one is its apparent simplicity. The Four Riders, the Seven Vials, the Whore of Babylon exist only within the conceptual framework of the Revelation. The case of whiteness is different, as the color is present in our world and known to everybody. Our familiarity with it, however, does not really help us in interpreting its role in the Revelation. The abundance of the obvious conceals the mysterious, and Melville's whiteness is used in much the same way. The role of this color in *Moby Dick* has drawn the attention of numerous scholars,[7] though its connection with the Book of Revelation has not been sufficiently explained. Most interpretations concentrate on the famous chapter 42, "The Whiteness of the Whale," which provides most clues to Melville's philosophy of whiteness. Lawrence Thompson makes a point in *Melville's Quarrel with God* that "the ambiguities and equivocations" of this chapter "should be recognized . . . as stylistic devices for deceptively masking Melville's own dark and heretical convictions," and goes on to argue that "the chapter is so contrived as to shift the balance progressively further away from the benevolent aspects of white and progressively nearer to the malevolent aspects of white."[8] While such a dynamic approach would not be unexpected in *Moby Dick*, it seems to focus on a mistaken juxtaposition. The chapter's opening sentence reads: "What the white whale was to Ahab, has been hinted; what, at times, he was to me, as yet remains unsaid" (p. 162), and the discussion of the relative meanings of whiteness is but another aspect of the Ahab-Ishmael opposition. To Ahab, Moby Dick is first of all a whale; to Ishmael, Moby Dick is first of all white. Ahab, himself a very complex personality, refuses to acknowledge any ambiguity in his pursuit of the whale, and treats it as an object that has to be destroyed. Ishmael, on the other hand, is much less a man of action than of intellect. He is capable of at least recognizing the inherent complexities and contradictions involved in the drama. He begins his analysis by enumerating some of the qualities that whiteness seems to convey. For that purpose he builds an elaborate construction where statements of positive evaluation are all preceded by repeated "though's" and finally juxtaposed by "there yet lurks an elusive something in the innermost idea of this hue, which strikes . . . of panic to the soul" (p. 163). Ishmael attempts, then, to reveal the hidden nature of this contradiction, yet his efforts are meaningfully futile. He looks for various creatures whose specific appeal could result from their whiteness, and the author's direct comments, included in footnotes (pp. 163-64), corroborate Ishmael's observations. With all this, however, Ishmael fails to penetrate the mystery of whiteness, and the final paragraph of the chapter is sorrowfully banal. Conclusions such as that "in essence whiteness is not so much a color as the visible absence of color, and at the same time the concrete of all colors" (p. 169) not only bring Ishmael no closer to the heart of the mystery, but are in fact uncomfortably reminiscent of Ahab's focus on the material rather than the spiritual. The final "Wonder ye then at the fiery hunt?" should thus be understood as Ishmael's acknowledgment of his own helplessness, combined with a desire to convey to the reader the need for further pursuit, rather than as his conviction that he has understood what it is in the whiteness of Moby Dick that generates such an urge.

Once again we are thus reminded of why Ahab is destroyed while Ishmael is not. "Whiteness," according to Melville, "is . . . the very veil of the Christian's Deity" (p. 169), and human beings should make a conscious effort at understanding the nature of the Divine Mystery without, however, ever being able to do so. In his arrogance Ahab not only believes that he has grasped the significance of the white whale: he also completely disregards it, concentrating instead on his own, personal relation to it. It is easy to misconstrue Ahab's (and Melville's) intentions, as George R. Creeger does when he says that "if white is the symbol of God, it is also the symbol of death; and the conclusion, toward which Melville has been moving, is that God Himself is dead."[9] Even if we disregard the obvious mistake in this syllogism, to conclude that whiteness represents God and at the same time that God is dead is to miss the basic assumption of *Moby Dick*. If Ahab's and Ishmael's quest is indeed a quest for God, which it very well may be, then their respective fates are the best proof that God is not dead. Ahab, who both misunderstands and challenges the sacred, shares the fate of Satan, while Ishmael survives the final destruction, apparently in recognition of his efforts to understand the transcendental and keep the faith despite his inability to comprehend its mystery. Ishmael's defeat comes in the form of a failure to understand the meaning of whiteness, but he continues his search, and his persistence may be rewarded with achieving the only true understanding of whiteness, which comes to those who will stand in white robes at the great white throne.

Ahab will never reach this point. His test came when he first encountered Moby Dick and lost a leg. By reacting with the desire for revenge, he failed the test. This is made clear when Melville draws on the story of Job in describing the whale:

Is this the creature of whom it was once so triumphantly said—"Canst thou fill his skin with barbed irons? or his head with fishspears? The sword of him that layeth at him cannot hold, the spear, the dart, not the habergeon: he esteemeth iron as straw; the arrow cannot make him flee; darts are counted as stubble; he laugheth at the shaking of a spear!'' (p. 309)

Job was commended by the Lord not only because his faith did not waiver, but also because he said "the right thing" to God, and Ahab fails on both counts. He does so, however, fully aware of the consequences. His pursuit of Moby Dick and his attempts to kill it, like his efforts to convince his crew that he can control the lightnings and the fire, are acts openly defiant of God. It is during the same scene of Ahab's rebellion that Ishmael is reminded of "God's burning fingers [that] has been laid on the ship; when His 'Mene, Mene, Tekel, Upharsin' has been woven into the shrouds and the cordage" (p. 433). In the conceptual framework of the apocalypse, Ahab can perhaps be most accurately described as the Beast of Revelation. Such an interpretation was first proposed by Michael T. Gilmore, who based his argument on few textual correlations; but a similar thesis can also be proved true on a higher level of symbolic representation.[10] Ahab declares war on God, but does so as a part of God's design. He is meant to provide a polarizing alternative, as well as to appear powerful, deceivingly attractive, and almost irresistible. What is more, Melville's own fear of the End, so convincingly portrayed, not only made him juxtapose Ahab with Ishmael, who provides hope, but also led him to have the latter saved by the *Rachel*. When the Lord heard the Biblical Rachel weep for her children, he assured her that "they shall come again from the land of the enemy ... to their own border" (Jer. 31:16-17). The children of Israel had been punished for their sovereigns' sins, but were ultimately allowed to return; the crew of the *Pequod* is also punished for their leader's acts, but this time only those who have clearly distanced themselves from him can hope for salvation.

The nature of this detachment is treated by Melville in a rather unusual manner. When Ahab makes the crew take the oath to pursue and kill the white whale, Ishmael does not refrain from doing so: "I, Ishmael, was one of that crew; my shouts had gone up with the rest; my oath had been welded with theirs. . . . A wild, mystical, sympathetic feeling was in me;" yet the sentence between these two reads: " . . . and stronger I shouted, and more did I hammer and clinch my oath, because of the dread in my soul" (p. 153). Ishmael alone is able to see the truth through the collective ceremony so skillfully manipulated by Ahab:

Who does not feel the irresistible arm drag? What skiff in tow of a seventy-four can stand still? For one, I gave myself up to the abandonment of the time and the place; *but while yet all a-rush to encounter the whale, could see nought in that brute but the deadliest ill.* (p. 162; emphasis added)

That last sentence, immediately preceding the "Whiteness of the Whale" chapter, explains not only Ishmael's survival but Melville's whole concept of evil: those are not the sinners who let themselves be carried away by momentary emotions, but rather those who fail to recognize the nature of the devil after emotions subside. Melville believes that "evil is an integral part of the cosmos itself,"[11] but even if it is indeed Manichean rather than Augustinian, man can and should oppose it, as this is the only way to salvation.

The middle of the nineteenth century was a period when feelings of achievement and satisfaction were mixed with anxiety about the future. But it was also, on a different plane, a period when man's control over his universe seemed to be a real possibility, when scientific discoveries made such control appear not only feasible, but imminent. Melville's treatment of the apocalypse proceeded along the same lines: while God's control over the transcendental could not be challenged, man was given the chance to establish his own place in God's design. Yet at the same time Melville's ideas ran counter to the intellectual and emotional mainstream of his times. By claiming that only those who actively seek their own salvation deserve it, he implied that a great majority does not. This contradicted the optimistic spirit of the period, as did his apparent stress on catastrophe rather than salvation—apparent because Melville's real interest focused on salvation, on the emergence of a new world. Melville's anxieties and conflicts were understood only decades later, by generations that discovered anew that the ultimate sense of the dreadful act of destruction lies in the miraculous prospect of renewal.

NOTES

1. Leslie A. Fiedler, *Love and Death in the American Novel*, p. 522.

2. Minor, yet meaningful, evidence of this is the fact that the original London edition (published simultaneously with the American one) left out the book's "Epilogue," crucial for its apocalyptic message.

3. See, for instance, Michael T. Gilmore, *The Middle Way: Puritanism and Ideology in American Romantic Fiction*, pp. 140-41, or Dayton Grover Cook, "The Apocalyptic Novel: *Moby Dick* and *Doktor Faustus*," pp. 171-73.

4. R.W.B. Lewis, *Trials of the Word*, p. 208.

5. Herman Melville, *Moby Dick*, p. 440. Subsequent references in parentheses are to this edition.

6. Nathalia Wright, *Melville's Use of the Bible*.

7. For a competent summary of critical opinions, see Khalil Husni, "The Whiteness of the Whale: A Survey of Interpretations, 1851-1970," pp. 210-21.

8. Lawrence Thompson, *Melville's Quarrel with God*, p. 194.

9. George Creeger, "The Symbolism of Whiteness in Melville's Prose Fiction," p. 155.

10. Gilmore, *The Middle Way*, p. 141.

11. R. E. Watters, "Melville's Metaphysics of Evil," p. 173.

3

MARK TWAIN, OR, AMBIGUITIES

The last two decades of the nineteenth century in America were a period of confusion and uncertainty. There were many hopeful signs: major industries flourished, bringing steel production and the expansion of railroad facilities to new heights; the flour and meat industries produced enough food not only for the domestic market but also for export to Europe; startling new inventions, such as the automobile, created bright prospects for progress, while earlier technological miracles, such as electric power and the telephone, began to influence the American lifestyle. At the same time, however, there were also signs of uneasiness as to what the future might bring: the depression of 1884, the panic of 1893, or the Silver Campaign Depression could be interpreted as warnings that technological and industrial progress might at some point lead to a disaster of unimaginable magnitude. The political scene was no more reassuring. Economic expansion was accompanied by immense corruption in the federal and local governments, and foreign policy led to yet another military conflict, the Spanish-American War. Moreover, increasingly frustrated and aggressive forces of protest were more and more conspicuous among farmers and in rapidly growing cities.

The anxieties, contradictions, hopes, and extravagances of the period have been among the favorite subjects of social and cultural history. They were also portrayed, with perhaps unmatched accuracy, by their great chronicler, Mark Twain. He not only actively participated in the frenzies of the period but also, through his writings, preserved the spirit of the times and strongly influenced their appraisal both by his contemporaries and by later generations. The existing body of Twain scholarship testifies to the breadth of social criticism contained in his works. At the same time, it is only fair to say that Twain was not primarily preoccupied with general philosophical ideas. When they appear in his works, they are expressed through socially oriented fiction, and are usually subordinated to it. One such idea that obliquely found its way into Twain's fiction is the concept of the apocalypse. Even though related images kept appearing in Twain's fiction, he did not fully devote any of his books to the subject of the apocalypse. Yet interest in such "final" themes increased with time, and his two late works, *A Connecticut Yankee in King Arthur's Court* and *The Mysterious Stranger*, can be said to have incorporated the apocalyptic structure as the main conceptual guideline hidden behind their ostensibly adventurous plots.

A Connecticut Yankee,[1] the earlier of the two, may be read as a simple story which combines the elements of Arthurian legend with the perennial myth of an omnipotent time traveller, who can change the course of events by using the knowledge he brings from the future. Behind this facade, however, lies a much deeper story, which ultimately deals with the birth and destruction of the world—even though *A Connecticut Yankee* is not a purely apocalyptic novel. In fact, many of its elements are characteristic of a related genre, the nineteenth-century American utopian novel, the best example of which is probably Ignatius Donnelly's *Caesar's Column*. *A Connecticut Yankee* combines to some extent the features of the apocalyptic novel with those of the utopian novel, but the latter are altered in order to accommodate the requirements of the former. Utopian novels are, as a rule, set in the future so that their contents cannot be disconfirmed through comparison with the present reality. While apocalyptic novels could not survive such comparison either, their time structure is less rigorous, and more diversified conventions have been adopted in order to reconcile the need for a narrative structure with the fact that nobody can live through the destruction and describe it. In *A Connecticut Yankee* the convention takes the form of placing the story outside a definable time frame. While the novel's first time plane is that of the late nineteenth century (when M. T. meets a stranger in Warwick Castle, learns about his adventures, and sees him die), the essential time structure is provided by King Arthur's court. It existed ostensibly in the sixth century, but as King Arthur and his knights belong primarily to the sphere of fantasy, not history, the novel is set outside historical time, in a chronological "black hole."

This is how the readers see the time structure of *A Connecticut Yankee*. For Hank Morgan, the book's main character, however, the existence of King Arthur's court is very real, and he establishes his identity there through a series of situations which are usually referred to as "apocalyptic." In an early scene the prospect of Morgan's death is connected with, and averted by, a phenomenon that appears frequently in popular apocalyptic imagery: a solar eclipse. By being able to foretell it, Morgan "prophesies" the end of the world, which he claims can be avoided only if his own life is spared. Hank is pardoned and "makes" the sun return, but the real meaning of the scene is that when Hank "stops" the sun, he symbolically separates himself not only from the conventional time structure, but also from solar time.

Another apocalyptic element concerns the fact that while Hank is described as a very skillful worker, his specialty is making mortal weapons of all kinds. At one point a co-worker hits him on the head with a crowbar, after which "the world went out in darkness, and [he] didn't feel anything more, and didn't know anything at all" (p. 21). He wakes up at King Arthur's court, but at the end of the book he is again found unconscious—first by Clarence in the sixth century, then by M. T. in the nineteenth, and he dies without coming to.

More such "apocalyptic" images can be found in the novel,[2] and they convey the same message: the world of *A Connecticut Yankee* exists independently of our reality and in this sense can be considered "new." The same point is argued by David Ketterer who, however, goes on to say that "Hank escapes death at the stake by fire or, in symbolic terms, survives the apocalypse and successfully enters the new world."[3] This statement seems to be imprecise in at least two points. First, no apocalypse occurs when Hank is chained to the stake; while the crowd believes the end is coming, the meaning of Hank's "miracle" is that he is capable of averting the catastrophe, not surviving it. Second, if this scene is to be interpreted as an apocalyptic end of the world, Hank's return to the nineteenth century cannot be interpreted in the same conceptual framework. Instead, it seems that if the novel is to be interpreted in apocalyptic terms, the events at King Arthur's court should be analyzed as preliminary to, not a consequence of, the apocalypse. The premillennial character of what is happening in the novel is further proved by the fact that King Arthur's subjects are offered a chance to reverse their ways and earn salvation. Initially most of them do, but they are not persistent enough: they turn around again and attack Hank. The punishment is swift and cruel, but also vain. "Those who do not want it, cannot be saved," Mark Twain seems to be saying in what is perhaps his characteristic mixture of the rational and the transcendental.

However, when Hank brings the offer of salvation, he encounters not only passive resistance from the "masses," but also a much more formidable opposition from Merlin. Any interpretation of the text has to explain the relation between these two men, yet this is also where we confront the book's fundamental ambiguity. From Hank's point of view (and this is the only perspective offered by the book's first-person narrative), Merlin is the personification of all that is conservative, mean, and insincere. He stands in the way of Hank's social reforms, pretends to possess secret knowledge, and is jealous of Hank's accomplishments. When the Messiah comes and brings happiness and prosperity, Merlin emerges as his chief adversary, ready to sacrifice the well-being of the people in order to preserve his reign over them. Seen through Hank's eyes, Merlin is a satanic figure.

This conclusion, however, is based on the assumption that Hank is himself an embodiment of good, and that his main concern is to save people. Hank believes that this is really the case, but from a less subjective perspective the juxtaposition of Hank and Merlin does not seem to be so clearly defined. First of all, Merlin is a defender and a mainstay of the established system which Hank, an impostor, tries to abolish. Furthermore, one cannot consider Arthur's court a seat of all evil. There are cruelty, injustice, stupidity, and insincerity in Merlin's England, but Hank's own nineteenth-century alternative is not any better. For any corrupt structure that Hank tries to eliminate, he can name two in his own society. Merlin has every reason to suspect and oppose the newcomer, and he would be justified in believing that Hank is Satan, or Satan's messenger. It is actually surprising that Merlin restrains himself from voicing such judgements. One explanation could be that while Hank is more successful, they both use similar methods, and accusations could backfire. Unfortunately, Merlin's unwillingness to challenge the source of Hank's power results in obscuring the essence of their conflict, which is the opposition between spirit and technology, or, in Henry Adams' terms, between Virgin and Dynamo. Merlin may be a pitiful sorcerer, unable to perform any miracles, but he has faith in his vocation. Hank is infinitely more efficient and has little trouble accomplishing even the most complicated tasks, but he knows that neither magic nor faith is involved in the process. He is a technician, who skillfully applies whatever technology he has learned, but is very cynical about what he is doing. This difference in attitude is perhaps best exemplified by the scene in which Hank restores the Holy Fountain. Having first mended the leak, Hank then prepares for a spectacular, and completely superfluous, performance. Merlin, on the other hand, has failed to make his own spells work and can only hope that Hank will not be successful either. At no point, however, does he question the validity of the procedure. He even warns Hank about the danger involved in trying to perform the miracle:

"Ye wit that he that would break this spell must know that spirit's name?"
"Yes, I know his name."
"And wit you also that to know it skills not of itself, but ye must likewise pronounce it? Ha-ha! Knew ye that?"
"Yes, I knew that, too."
"You had that knowledge! Art a fool? Are ye minded to utter that name and die?"
"Utter it? Why certainly. I would utter it if it was Welsh."
"Ye are even a dead man, then."   (p. 287)

Undaunted, Hank proceeds with his plans, and utters the dreaded word. He then ignites the fireworks, waits for a "mighty groan of terror," and turns on the water. His technological knowledge has worked again; moreover, it also destroys Merlin, who alone "recognizes" the enormity of Hank's accomplishment:

He had caved in and gone down like a landslide when I pronounced that fearful name, and had never come to since. He never had heard that name before,— neither had I—but to him it was the right one. . . . He never could under stand how I survived it, and I didn't tell him. . . . Merlin spent three months working enchantments to try to find the deep trick of how to pronounce that name and outlive it. But he didn't arrive.   (p. 294)

Hank's triumph seems to be complete. He has intimidated Merlin, impressed the king, and conquered the crowd. He goes on to introduce new technological inventions. Even though both he and the king almost lose their lives trying to acquaint themselves with the customs of the country's common people, Hank's technological utopia is not far from completion.

And yet Hank fails. Just as his plan approaches the final stage, the Church puts the Interdict on him, and all but a handful of the most faithful followers desert him. One explanation of the Church's action is rather obvious and follows the pattern of social criticism contained in Twain's books: the hierarchy wanted to regain its influence, wealth, and power. According to this interpretation, the clergy would sacrifice people's happiness in order to protect their own interests. It seems, however, that *A Connecticut Yankee* is a more ambiguous novel than such an interpretation would indicate.

Hank's blueprint for progress called for a calculated program of social changes introduced through institutional reforms. It did not take into account people's need for moral guidance, and their preference of unjust spiritual leadership to the total lack of it. When the Church decided to declare war on Hank, it may have been defending mankind from the potentially destructive consequences of allowing technological progress to push aside higher values. Twain's ambiguous feelings should be judged against the background of the controversies of his own times: Henry Adams was not alone in his fears that the Dynamo was destroying the Virgin. Seen from this perspective, Hank represented not so much the bright prospects for man's future as a direct threat, posed by the Powers of Darkness, to his spiritual survival. The Church had thus a duty to stand up and fight, and the Battle of the Sand-Belt can be interpreted as the book's Armageddon, with the future of the world at stake.

The battle is certainly among Twain's most horrifying scenes. Over thirty thousand people are killed: electrocuted, drowned, shot. But the description of the slaughter is surprisingly detached, concerned more with the technical means of the genocide than with its ghastly effects. The reason is expressed clearly in the letter that Hank, as The Boss, sends to the enemy's troops:

You have no chance—none whatever. Reflect: we are well equipped, well fortified, we number 54. Fifty-four what? Men? No, *minds*—the capablest in the world; a force against which mere animal might may no more hope to prevail than may the idle waves of the sea hope to prevail against the granite barriers of England. (p. 558)

Yet the "animal might," or the knights of the kingdom, do not lose the battle against the self-confident power of technology. After they all die, their bodies form a deadly ring around the fortification, and those inside also perish. Moreover, Hank is stabbed by a dying knight, and while he is not fatally wounded, he is incapacitated and cannot defend himself against Merlin's last ploy. Helpless and pitiful in his earlier attempts, the magician performs his last trick faultlessly, and puts Hank to sleep for thirteen centuries. When Merlin, careless in his triumph, touches a charged wire and also dies, the apocalyptic structure is brought to an end. The death of Hank, a false prophet (and thus, at least partially, an Antichrist figure), is followed by the death of the symbolic defender of the faith.

What remains on the ruins of the technological civilization is the people, "all England," as a disciple of Hank puts it. When they had shifted from full support of the reforms to the universal outcry of "Death to the Republic," Hank was shocked. What it signified, however, was a new beginning, a true rebirth of the people. Had they followed The Boss to the end, they could possibly have exchanged one form of oppression for another. By turning against him after some of the most unbearable burdens had been removed, "all England" became more free than ever before. In this sense *A Connecticut Yankee* can be said to possess at least a degree of optimism. It seems that this is also how the book was understood by Daniel Carter Beard, whose illustrations frequently interpret the text. His final drawing shows the figure of Death, terrifying yet visibly defeated, above which there appears a picture of a happy couple with a newly born child. Its obvious oversimplification aside, the fundamental meaning of the drawing clearly corresponds to traditional apocalyptic imagery, in which rebirth follows the destruction and brings eternal happiness.

Such moments of hope cannot dispel the prevailing mood of alienation and waste. Yet we must not forget that death is always a part of the apocalyptic structure, whose final meaning depends on whether annihilation leads to regeneration, or not. In this sense, and recognizing all its ambiguities, *A Connecticut Yankee* belongs to the tradition of "optimistic" apocalyptic structures, where regeneration is the final stage of the process. At the same time, the prevailing sense of transition, which resulted in increasing ambiguity, was perhaps more characteristic of late nineteenth-century fiction than of any other period in American literature. Twain was one of the most prominent exponents of these

uncertainties and his treatment of the apocalyptic theme testifies to the degree of his own indecisiveness.

If *A Connecticut Yankee* still belongs to the clearly identifiable tradition, Twain's late and unfinished novel, *The Mysterious Stranger*, cannot be so easily classified. "The Chronicle of Young Satan," the earliest version of *The Mysterious Stranger* (except for the very brief "St. Petersburg Fragment"), was written between 1897 and 1900.[4] While it can also be read as a children's story, significant parts of the novel originated in the tradition of literary apocalypse. Twain's working notes include references to "Your new Jerusalem & your pearly gates & so on" (B, p. 448; see also B, p. 418), and although the actual text does not contain direct allusions to the Book of Revelation, there are many elements in it that can be recognized as apocalyptic images. Probably the most conspicuous among them is the reign of Satan which is to precede the Last Judgement. His arrival is announced at the beginning of the book, even though the description of Satan ostensibly refers to the owner of the village of Eseldorf: "When [he] came it was as if the lord of the world had arrived, and had brought all the glories of its kingdoms along" (CYS, p. 36).

There is no further mention of this unnamed prince, but several pages later the local feast of the Assuaging of the Devil is described. It commemorates the day when a local prior outwitted the Devil and provided the community with a bridge without paying the customary price of one human soul. Moreover, the current parson, Father Adolf, is widely believed to have met Satan. Finally, the young narrator, Theodore Fischer, and his two companions are accosted by a young man, who first identifies himself as an angel, but later gives his name as Satan. The remaining part of the book is devoted to the presentation of Satan's philosophy and power. While the "Chronicle" remains to a large degree a children's story, and while the depth of its message should not be overestimated, Twain does employ a substantial number of apocalyptic images and is concerned with questions which have also been asked by other writers discussed in this study. In the words of Hyatt Waggoner:

Mark Twain lived the last fifteen years of his life ... think[ing] of man as a machine buffeted by an indifferent, if not hostile, mechanical universe. Such an outlook was not unique in his generation. The cold drafts of the new scientific doctrines were chilling the hearts of many men who had known the snugness of a God-centered, benevolent world.[5]

Despite common concerns, the difference between Twain and most writers of his generation was that for him even the world ruled by transcendental forces was not "benevolent," but hostile. Even though Satan's actions are as a rule determined by whims rather than by a scientific doctrine, the outcome is no more encouraging. One of the cruelest scenes of the book comes when Satan first creates and then destroys a whole community of humanlike creatures without so much as acknowledging their existence. When the boys try to persuade him not to kill those people, his reply is an indifferent "It is no matter, [I] can make more" (CYS, p. 52). Even when he yields to the children's requests and appears to be helping people, he is invariably inflicting new hardships upon them. On one occasion, for instance, he agrees to save somebody from immediate death; as a result of this, the unfortunate man is given time to commit major sins and ultimately goes to hell rather than to heaven, as he otherwise would have. Another such example is Father Peter, whom Satan entraps and sends to prison. When the boys beg for the delivery of the innocent priest, Satan agrees, and "liberates" the preacher by driving him insane. Father Peter's original fault, for which he was punished by his bishop, was to believe "that God was all goodness and would find a way to save *all* his poor human children" (CYS, p. 42). The "Chronicle" shows, however, that even if salvation is available at all, it is almost impossible to gain. Some people go to hell because they have led a sinful life, but others will be so punished because of an unfortunate circumstance: "If we had been an hour earlier the priest would have been in time to send that poor creature to heaven, but now he was gone down into the awful fires, to burn forever" (CYS, p. 76).

The main reason why the humans deserve all the punishment, both temporal and eternal, is their adherence to the Moral Sense:

"What is the moral sense, sir?"
[Father Peter] looked down surprised, over his great spectacles, and said—
"Why, it is the faculty which enables us to distinguish good from evil." . . .
"Is it valuable?"
"*Valuable*! Heavens, lad, it is the one thing that lifts man above the beasts that perish and makes him heir to immortality!" (CYS, p. 60)

. . .

[Men] have foolish little feelings, and foolish little vanities and impertinences and ambitions, their foolish little life is but a laugh, a sigh, and extinction; and they have no sense. Only the Moral Sense [said Satan]. (CYS, p. 113)

The Moral Sense is essentially the ability to tell good from evil. The apocalyptic structure of *Moby Dick* is based largely on the interaction between these values: whatever their personal preference, the novel's protagonists recognize the existence of the dichotomy as well as its implications. So do Theodore Fischer and his companions—until their belief is questioned, ridiculed, and finally rejected as a result of Satan's arguments. His criticism of the Moral Sense seems to be twofold. First, people's pride in possessing this unique quality is groundless, since what is good to some people is frequently harmful or destructive to others. Second, even if they can distinguish between right and wrong, people are easily persuaded to abandon their Moral Sense when promised personal gains, or when tempted by a charming young man, for whom Satan passes.

The children realize Satan's destructive influence, but they cannot help being fascinated by his power, just as the adults, who are not aware of his real identity, appreciate his unusual gifts. He is not only capable of performing tricks and miracles, but also displays power that makes people willingly submit to him. This uncritical acceptance of Satan, which results in people breaking their vows, betraying friends, and committing harmful deeds, is the best expression of Twain's disillusionment and bitterness. He offers no alternative to Satan's reign: even those who free themselves from it can do so only because Satan has decided to let them go. People themselves are unable to pursue good instead of evil consistently, despite, or perhaps because of, their claim to be the only creatures who possess the Moral Sense.

With the criticism of the Moral Sense being essential for understanding Twain's message, all ambiguities in the presentation of this concept reflect upon the structure of the whole book, and Twain is not consistent in his treatment of Satan, the main critic of the Moral Sense. "The Chronicle of Young Satan" was conceived as a children's story, where "the willing suspension of disbelief" encourages even the most extraordinary constructions, and at the same time as an apocalyptic picture of the world, where certain conventions have to be observed. As a character in a book for children, Satan can be charming, well meaning, and reliable, but as an archetypal figure, he is deceitful, dangerous, and untrustworthy. In the former capacity he can serve as the author's mouthpiece. When he lashes out at the Moral Sense, he expresses Twain's own dissatisfaction with the human race. As an archetypal deceiver, however, Satan cannot be trusted and, consequently, his criticism defeats itself. The final outcome is that the concepts of right and wrong, of good and evil, become relative, and the apocalyptic structure, based largely on such oppositions, collapses. The manuscript lacks a clear conceptual framework and when it is abruptly abandoned, with Satan involved in yet another cheap trick, this seems like the only possible ending of a literary project without its own "moral sense." It seems, too, that Twain himself must have been aware of the inconsistencies in the story, for he was simultaneously working on another version of the novel presumably free from the discrepancies of "The Chronicle of Young Satan."

"Schoolhouse Hill" was begun toward the end of 1898. Twain moved the action from an Austrian village to the familiar location of St. Petersburg, Missouri: Tom Sawyer and Huck Finn both appear in the story. Yet this version never really takes off either. Despite the author's efforts, the inconsistencies contained in the "Chronicle" are even more conspicuous in "Schoolhouse Hill," which on the one hand follows the mood of *The Adventures of Tom Sawyer*, with its familiar collection of school pranks, and on the other employs the archetypal figure of Satan. Trying to reconcile the discrepancy, Twain makes his "little Satan" (referred to as Forty-four) a rebel figure who not only saves people from dying without the last rites and going to hell, but who also opposes Satan: Forty-four goes so far as to claim he is not a devil.

What is most interesting about Forty-four is his explanation of the origin of evil. Contrary to the general understanding of the apple as the source of the *knowledge* of good and evil, Forty-four believes that it was the source of the *"disposition to DO evil"* (SH, p. 216). Evil itself appeared only after Satan himself had tasted the fruit: "There was no tempter until my father ate of the fruit himself and became one. Then he tempted other angels and they ate of it also; then Adam and the woman" (SH, p. 215).

This was followed by the creation of hell and, subsequently, "through the sacrifice made . . . by the son of God, the Savior" (SH, p. 215), heaven appeared. Such an interpretation can lead to a fundamental reconsideration of the opposition between good and evil, as well as to a re-evaluation of the concept of the apocalypse, including the meaning of the Last Judgement. Clearly enough, the framework of "Schoolhouse Hill" could not sustain so formidable a task, and Twain abandoned the story in the middle of the sixth chapter. William M. Gibson goes a step further when he assumes that "perhaps certain inherent contradictions within the character of 44 and in his projected actions proved too great for Twain to resolve."[6] Yet despite failing twice, Twain kept trying, and in the years that followed he came close to completing another, and possibly final, version of the manuscript, known as "No. 44, The Mysterious Stranger."

The action is again set in Austria, though more than two hundred years earlier than in the "Chronicle," in 1490. The village is again called Eseldorf ("a donkey place"), but the cast of characters has been changed almost completely. The Satan of this version, called 44, is not above performing unsophisticated tricks, but he does not interfere with people's destiny the way he did in the "Chronicle." While this may seem to be simply a difference in form, it actually reflects a basic change in Twain's *Weltanschauung*. In reply to Theodore's question, the young Satan of the earlier version offers the following view of man's dependence on God's will:

"Does God order the career?"
"Foreordain it? No. The man's circumstances and environment order it. His first act determines the second and all that follow after." (CYS, p. 115)

When, however, August Feldner pleads for the life of an old woman about to die at the stake, No. 44 replies: "It is not so written, . . . that which is not foreordained will not happen" (MS, p. 325).

This is not so much a result of Satan's decreased power as an expression of Twain's diminished belief that man's environment, or natural forces, take precedence over transcendental powers. Was Twain so disappointed with the scientific interpretations of man's fate that he looked to the supernatural during the last period of his life? *The Mysterious Stranger* does not fully answer this question, but it certainly seems to confirm Waggoner's opinion, quoted earlier, that at the time he wrote the book Twain vacillated between the two outlooks, no longer certain which one had more merit.

Further evidence of Twain's ambivalence is provided by his treatment of the Last Judgement, an indispensable element of the apocalyptic structure. In one of the book's final scenes, 44 calls the Assembly of the Dead. He summons the dead from all epochs and areas and makes them march "ten thousand abreast" in front of bewildered, but impressed, August:

[The hall] was a vast and lofty corridor, now, and stretched away for miles and miles and the Procession drifted solemnly down it sorrowfully clacking, losing definiteness gradually, and finally fading out in the far distances, and melting from sight. (MS, p. 401)

The Assembly, however, is never transformed into the Judgement scene: nobody is granted salvation, and nobody is sent to hell, as if the purpose of the whole procession is limited to making an impression on August. It obviously is not, but the real explanation is even more radical. Immediately following the march, 44 tells the startled August, "*Nothing exists save empty space—and you!*" (MS, p. 404). The implications of such a solipsistic conclusion reach far beyond understanding the meaning of *The Mysterious Stranger*. Good and evil, moral judgement, and the apocalypse itself are all social phenomena which are relevant only insofar as their frame of reference includes relationships among people, or between men and transcendental powers. Solipsism cannot be reconciled with these concepts, and 44's statement has to be interpreted as an unconvincing solution offered by the writer who could not find an unequivocal answer to confusing existential questions. The fate of the *Mysterious Stranger* manuscripts and Twain's failure to complete the book certainly testify to his diminishing creative powers. On a different plane, his inability to finish the novel was a result of the disappearance of spiritual guidelines which had in the past made it possible for writers not only to present their visions of the apocalypse, but also to use them to formulate their own artistic and moral credo.

NOTES

1. Samuel Langhorne Clemens, *A Connecticut Yankee in King Arthur's Court*. Subsequent references in parentheses are to this edition.
2. Cf. David Ketterer, *New Worlds for Old: The Apocalyptic Imagination*, pp. 213-32.
3. Ibid., p. 215.
4. Samuel Langhorne Clemens, *Mark Twain's Mysterious Stranger Manuscripts*. Gibson's edition will be used in this chapter and, while the book's

pagination is continuous, abbreviations will be used to indicate the version quoted: CYS for "The Chronicle of Young Satan"; SH for "Schoolhouse Hill"; MS for "No. 44, the Mysterious Stranger"; A and B for "Appendix A" and "Appendix B."

5. Hyatt Howe Waggoner, "Science in the Thought of Mark Twain," p. 357.

6. William M. Gibson, Introduction to *Mysterious Stranger Manuscripts*, p. 9.

APOCALYPSE AS A BLACK EXPERIENCE: RALPH ELLISON'S *INVISIBLE MAN*

For almost the entire first half of the twentieth century, American fiction was characterized by the dominance of the realistic-naturalistic tradition. Some of William Faulkner's or John Dos Passos' works notwithstanding, the American novel of this period was much more indebted to the nineteenth-century English or French realists than to James Joyce or Marcel Proust. The acceptance of Faulkner in the late 1940s followed the recognition of his genius in Europe and did not necessarily prove the receptiveness of the American public to his mode of writing; John Hawkes, one of the most original creative talents in America, did not find such support abroad and remained a writers' writer. In this context, the appearance of Ralph Ellison's *Invisible Man* in 1952 was a literary event of great consequence. The book is more than the most important black novel in America, or even ''one of the greatest post-war American novels.'' It is a book that signifies the end of one literary tradition and the arrival of another. It is a precursor of a new mode of writing that was strongly indebted to the tradition of nineteenth-century symbolism in American literature.

As is usually the case with innovative works of art, *Invisible Man* retains some characteristics of the period that it helps bring to an end. A great part of the plot can be discussed in purely realistic terms, with the narrator growing up in the South, entering college, going to New York, and participating in the emerging black movements. Obviously, such an interpretation would not do justice to Ellison's message, which is conveyed not so much through the vicissitudes of the narrator as through the symbolism of the novel's apocalyptic structure. Moreover, this structure differs radically from previous literary realizations of the concept.

The fundamental difference between apocalypses in earlier religious systems and the Judaeo-Christian apocalypse is that the former are cyclic phenomena, and the latter is linear. Consequently, American literary apocalypses are almost invariably linear, with the plot leading toward one-time destruction, followed by rebirth. Some authors—Robert Coover, for instance—may have been attracted by the possibility of the cyclic repetition of apocalyptic events, but the American literary apocalypse is characteristically a linear structure. *Invisible Man* thus stands alone in American literature as a novel which presents the cyclic apocalypse. The book develops through a series of cyclic sub-structures, all of which possess characteristic apocalyptic features. The life of the unnamed narrator uncoils not as a continuity, but in semi-independent phases, which all end in a symbolic death. The hero is then ''reborn'' and begins a new cycle:

Ralph Ellison's book . . . takes its hero through a series of initiatory episodes from which he emerges a new man, an individual with the godlike power to create. The pattern is generally that of a quest for identity, the birth of the individual out of the chaos of man's manifold potential.... *Invisible Man* is cyclical in form and resembles the ritual cycle it re-enacts.[1]

The unprecedented structure of *Invisible Man* is congruent with its main thematic line: the opposition between whites and blacks. It is almost as if by rejecting the tradition that goes back to the Puritans, Ellison wanted to express the separateness of American black culture. Despite its subordination to white culture, it has preserved its own identity. Yet this steadfastness has also meant that the lines between the cultures have grown ever more evident. The young man who is the narrator of the novel does not initially recognize that the difference between the races is insurmountable. However, in the process of the gradual discovery of his identity through a series of apocalyptic structures, the futility of his efforts to ignore the difference becomes obvious.

He is never referred to by name, which is ostensibly an expression of the white men's contempt for the blacks. Yet he is not altogether nameless. Just as *Moby Dick* opens by identifying the narrator—"Call me Ishmael"—the first sentence of Ellison's novel is "I am an invisible man."[2] This is how we know him throughout the book, but if "Invisible Man" passes for his name, his initials are "I. M." The opening phrase could thus read "I am I. M."—or "I am I'm." In other words, Ellison's hero is not unnamed: his name, rather than being individual, stands for all those who share his existential experience. We may remember that Everyman was not every man either, but rather a figure for those who came from the same cultural and religious background. Similarly, the opening existential declaration of Ellison's hero makes him the spokesman for the people of his cultural group.

In the historical period described in the novel, the American blacks were in the process of striving for recognition of their existence as full human beings. Only after the fact that "they were" was no longer questioned could they proceed to fight for their rights. Throughout this process, the relation between them and the whites was an adversary one. Consequently, if the apocalypse of *Invisible Man* deals with the rebirth of the black man, the satanic opponent he has to face and overcome is the white man.

The Invisible Man (as the novel's main character will be referred to here) was born in the South. He grew up in a world of white domination, which he fully endorsed. He was so immobilized by his willing subordination that he did not recognize the humiliation involved in the final episode of his childhood cycle, the battle royal. Apart from its description of the boy's meaningful passiveness, the scene is significant for its introduction of the two elements that mark the end of subsequent cycles in the Invisible Man's life: physical violence and sex. In terms of the apocalyptic structure, the former stands for death and destruction, while the latter symbolizes rebirth. In a demeaning and painful scene, the Invisible Man is made to fight with several other black boys. He is defeated, and physical violence signifies the end of the novel's first apocalyptic cycle. As to the sex symbol, the naked belly dancer is perhaps a crude personification of the rebirth concept, but in this respect she does not differ from other components of the scene. While the Invisible Man is fully aware of the inaccessibility of the white woman, her proximity makes him for the first time challenge the restraints of his condition: "Had the price of looking been blindness, I would have looked" (p. 16). But his rebellion remains in the subconscious. He does not realize that he can break out of his constraints, and when the first period of his life is brought to an end, he is unable to make the new cycle significantly different.

When he begins his new life, it is almost as if he were entering the promised land:

It was a beautiful college. The buildings were old and covered with vines and the roads gracefully winding, lined with hedges and wild roses that dazzled the eyes in the summer sun. Honeysuckle and purple wisteria hung heavy from the trees and white magnolias mixed with their scents in the beehumming air. . . . How the grass turned green in the springtime and how the mocking birds fluttered their tails and sang, how the moon shone down on the buildings, how the bell in the chapel tower rang out the precious short-lived hours; how the girls in bright summer dresses promenaded the grassy lawn. (p. 27)

He begins this cycle accepting unquestioningly the position of the white man, but he has also learned that a black man can achieve a position of respectability and authority, as did the Founder and Dr. Bledsoe. The Invisible Man can thus imagine finding satisfaction and happiness for himself without upsetting the existing system. The promise of a new earth seems to be very real.

When the catastrophe comes, it is again preceded by physical violence and associated with sex. The Invisible Man thoughtlessly takes one of the college's white trustees, Mr. Norton, to the house of a local Negro, Jim Trueblood. Trueblood has recently committed an incestuous act and has made both his wife and daughter pregnant. When Trueblood tells his story, Mr. Norton is deeply shocked. He expresses his reaction in apocalyptic terms ("You have looked upon chaos and are not destroyed!" [p. 40]), yet it is not he, but the Invisible Man whose world is about to be destroyed. Trying to prevent Mr. Norton from having a heart attack, the boy drives him to a local bar, the Golden Day, which is also a house of ill repute frequented by the patients of a nearby psychiatric institution. Mr. Norton's arrival is greeted with the proclamation that "already the Creator has come" (p. 61), and a sequence of sex-related and violent events follows. While the patients almost kill their warden, the prostitutes try to seduce Mr. Norton and his guide. The Invisible Man finally manages to get back to the campus, but his dream of the new earth is over as he is dismissed from the college. He is mistreated again but he still does not understand the real nature of what is happening to him. His trust in the authority and the power of the white man remains intact.

He leaves the college hoping that his perseverance can help him return. The apocalyptic structure, however, can be a recurrent or a one-time event; it is not reversible. Once the Invisible Man enters a new reality, the old one is lost forever. Significantly, a new cycle opens with a sexual promise: an old black doctor tells him that if he is successful he "might even dance with a white girl!" (p. 117). The Invisible Man's arrival in New York indicates a fundamental change in the boy's life. While the passage from his home town to college was important, he remained in very similar cultural surroundings. The second change is much more momentous. New York is completely new territory for the Invisible Man, and he again believes it will be his promised land. The disillusionment comes when he learns of the content of the letter Dr. Bledsoe gave him: presumably to facilitate his search for a job in New York, but in fact to "Keep This Nigger-Boy Running." While the Invisible Man recognizes the supremacy of the white men, he thinks he can trust his own race, and Bledsoe's letter destroys this faith. When he subsequently applies for a job at Liberty Paints, he uses the name of one of the college's white trustees, Mr. Emerson. The ploy is successful and the Invisible Man is hired, but the symbolic breach with his own people and his reliance upon the white race is ominous and leads to another catastrophe.

As soon as the Invisible Man starts working, he is subjected to a series of abuses—verbal, moral, and finally physical. His first supervisor mistreats him for trying to be helpful. When he is transferred to another job, his new boss, Lucius Brockway, suspects him of trying to steal production secrets. The Invisible Man then stumbles into a union meeting, where he is accused of being a "fink," and as soon as he returns to Brockway, he is forced to fight the old man. It is all too clear that the Invisible Man has been alienated from the world around him, that he is rejected by everybody who can provide him with a measure of security. He is persecuted, but his persecution is part of the apocalyptic structure: while it leads to destruction, it will also bring purification and rebirth.

The destruction takes the form of an explosion in a factory basement. When it occurs, the Invisible Man experiences "a fall into space that seemed not a fall but a suspension." He is left "to sink to the center of a lake of heavy water and pause, transfixed and numb with the sense that [he] had lost irrevocably an important victory'' (p. 175). The victory that he has been denied would have been a success in the world he knows. By its standards the Invisible Man has failed. He has not become another Booker T. Washington; he has been rejected by the black educators; and he has not established his own identity. The explosion destroys the man who has been unable to meet the demands imposed upon him by others. When he is reborn, he becomes a man capable of establishing his own frame of reference: ''the descent into 'the heart of darkness,' as a movement of the spirit, as a way of coming to terms with the self . . . is a stratagem of renewal that has its own dignity and positiveness and moral validity.''[3]

The Invisible Man's passage from his former existence to the next occurs during the medical treatment he receives after the explosion. His physical condition is diagnosed as good, but he complains that something has happened to his head, and that he has got ''a burning eye inside.'' In order to ''get him started again'' doctors apply ''pressure in the proper degrees to the major centers of nerve control,'' and hope to achieve a ''complete change of personality'' (p. 180). They succeed, and it is easy to misinterpret their role in the Invisible Man's rebirth. The white doctors force some changes in his brain through mechanical means, but the transformation is possible only because he has a potential for it. When after the treatment he is told, ''Well, boy, it looks as though you're cured.... You're a new man'' (p. 186), the statement is unintentionally ironical. While he is a new man in the sense that he has gone through another destruction-rebirth process, he certainly is not ''cured.'' On the contrary, he is really ''sick'' now because he is able to rebel. The doctors do not understand the change and continue to apply their own standards, rather than his. As a measure of a successful therapy they insist that the Invisible Man remember his name. They do not realize that his name has never really mattered to him. It had been given to his ancestors by a white owner, but it did not help them or himself become visible. By the doctors' standards, the Invisible Man is a cured patient and can be released from their care; by his own measure, he has just entered a new reality. He leaves the hospital and a new phase of the apocalyptic structure begins.

This beginning is different than the previous ones. In the past a certain continuity was observed, and the Invisible Man could be manipulated into believing that the changes were reversible. This time he realizes that there is no way back, and he is fully aware of entering a completely new period of life. He feels that he does not belong even to the most immediate past ("The moment I entered the bright, buzzing lobby of Men's House I was overcome by a sense of alienation and hostility" [p. 194]), and he symbolically breaks away from his previous conditioning by physically abusing a man he thinks is Dr. Bledsoe. He also moves to a guest house run by a black woman called Mary, who provides him with motherly care. The significance of this is almost too obvious, particularly in that the Invisible Man returns to Harlem after the major apocalyptic transformation from which he has emerged with a new consciousness.

Even though he does not at first recognize his new role, and is inclined to think that he "ha[s] no contacts and . . . believe[s] in nothing" (p. 197), the Invisible Man soon becomes aware that

somewhere beneath the load of the emotion-freezing ice which my life had conditioned my brain to produce, a spot of black anger glowed and threw off a hot red light of such intensity that had Lord Kelvin known of its existence, he would have had to revise his measurements. A remote explosion had occurred somewhere, . . . and it had caused the ice cap to melt and shift the slightest bit. But that bit, that fraction, was irrevocable. (p. 197)

As the ice melts away, the Invisible Man goes through the final stage of the purification process which will eventually enable him to fulfill his mission. Walking down a Harlem street, he encounters a yam vendor. He buys a yam, an action that until now he would have considered unbecoming, and suddenly realizes that

it was exhilarating. I no longer had to worry about who saw me or about what was proper. To hell with all that. . . . If only someone who had known me at school or at home would come along and see me now. How shocked they'd be! I'd push them into a side street and smear their faces with the peel. (p. 200)

This is the symbolic end of the Invisible Man's old life, and immediately following is the eviction scene, which is when his new life begins. An elderly couple is being thrown out of their apartment for being unable to pay the rent. The Invisible Man joins the gathering crowd, and as he goes through the couple's meager belongings, he finds FREE PAPERS. Looking at the document, he suddenly realizes that slavery has more than one meaning, that being free in the eyes of the law is not the same as being a really free man. A man is free only when he does not feel bound by limitations imposed by others. Having just shed his own restraints, the Invisible Man suddenly finds himself in the role of a leader. He addresses the crowd and manages to arouse it, but he is unable to give it direction. He does not even know what he wants to accomplish. He first tries to stop the people who attack the police, but when they disregard his appeals, he joins them. With his old obedient self destroyed, the reborn Invisible Man must learn what his objectives are before he can become a true leader.

This is when he is accosted by Brother Jack and asked to join the Brotherhood. He hesitates, perhaps unwilling to give up his new freedom, but eventually agrees and thus fully enters the second major phase of his life. Again, both violence and sex accompany the process. First, the eviction scene leads to bloodshed. Later, when the Invisible Man attends a Brotherhood social gathering, he is asked to dance with an attractive white woman. It is an event of extraordinary significance to him. He compares it with one of the most important moments in the history of his family, which also symbolizes the black man's deprivation:

The thing to do was to be prepared—as my grandfather had been when it was demanded that he quote the entire United States Constitution as a test of his fitness to vote. He had confounded them all by passing the test, although they still refused him the ballot. (p. 239)

What he does not realize is that by allowing himself to be fascinated with what is offered him he becomes vulnerable to manipulation and, ultimately, to another enslavement. He chooses to disregard not only an unpleasant racial incident ("How about a spiritual, Brother? ... *all* colored people sing" [pp. 236-237]) but also ambiguous comments that the scene draws ("*I* would never ask our colored brothers to sing, even though I love to hear them" [p. 238]). Even more significantly, he does not object to the scene that should have alerted him to the dangers of his new situation. It is clearly parallel to the earlier subordination procedures to which he was subjected.

I watched [Emma] reach into the bosom of her taffeta hostess gown and remove a white envelope.
    "This is your new identity," Brother Jack said. "Open it."
    Inside I found a name written on a slip of paper.

"That is your new name," Brother Jack said. "Start thinking of yourself by that name from this moment." (p. 235)

The enslavement process continues when the Invisible Man goes to a public Brotherhood meeting. He delivers a very effective speech whose arguments, rhythm, and tone resemble traditional Negro sermons. While the audience enthusiastically accepts the new speaker, his Brotherhood comrades harshly criticize the speech for individualism. The Invisible Man is told to begin a reeducation program with the organization's chief ideologue. Freedom, which he enjoyed ever so briefly, is definitely lost. In a sense his new captivity, being virtually self-imposed, is even more overwhelming and difficult to surmount. In terms of the apocalyptic structure, however, it is a desirable development. By "turning motion into direction" the Invisible Man, who has already displayed some Christ-like features, can confirm his position in the community, as well as identify his enemies in order to defeat them later.

The first task is relatively easy because he is almost immediately accepted by people. They trust him, and as they join the Brotherhood the ideology he preaches spreads around Harlem. The Invisible Man then proceeds to fulfill his other task, which is to expose and defeat his main foe. This is where he commits a fateful mistake. He is fully aware that the Brotherhood is not the only organized black movement in Harlem. Another group with a considerable following is led by Ras the Exhorter. His ideology includes several elements that the Invisible Man tries to disregard or impugn. Ras is black, and he feels proud of his skin color. He does not feel inferior to white men and would not let them mistreat him, which differs considerably from the Invisible Man's attitude, not only in the past, but also at present. Ras is primitive, cannot speak good English, and does not care about his manners, which annoys the Invisible Man almost as much as the contents of Ras' speeches. Finally, Ras capitalizes on the African origin of American blacks, and while the Invisible Man is interested in the life of Marcus Garvey (an old newspaper with a story about Garvey is among the documents he goes through before delivering his eviction speech), he disapproves of Garvey's ideas, as well as of Ras' primitive arguments:

"We sons of Mama Africa, you done forgot? You black, BLACK! You— *Godahm*, mahn!" he said, swinging the knife for emphasis. "You got bahd *hair*! You got thick *lips*! They say you *stink*! They hate you, mahn. You African. AFRICAN!" (p. 280)

Consequently, the Invisible Man mistakenly believes that Ras is his main enemy. He thinks that once Ras' misleading ideology is rejected, the united black people of Harlem will enter a period of a more satisfying life. He will not admit the possibility that Ras may be an ally, even if not specifically of the Brotherhood, at least of black people in general. What he refuses to accept is that the division can be drawn not along ideological lines, but along strictly racial ones. Yet the reality of *Invisible Man* is defined by race. With all temporary alliances and discords, the fundamental distinction between being black and being white cannot be overcome. For the Invisible Man as a Christ figure, the real enemy is the white people. He does not want to admit it—until the apocalypse comes and events convince him. But then it is too late, and the Invisible Man cannot emerge victorious from Armageddon.

The novel's final destruction begins for him with another sex scene, involving a white woman, Sybil, whose secret dream is to be raped by a black man. The sexual theme has come full circle: from the rigors of the deep South, where black men would not even talk about white women for fear of being accused of rape, to the liberal intellectuals in New York, where "interracial marriages are fashionable and women express their "liberation" through promiscuity. Even more important, the Invisible Man has also completed his own circle. Just as upon graduation he found himself forced to take part in the battle royal, he now believes he fights other black men for the sake of his race, and does not understand—until it is too late—that he is once again made to oppose his allies for the benefit of the white people.

When the Invisible Man returns to Harlem, he is again preoccupied with Ras. Ras the Exhorter has become Ras the Destroyer and has announced the final battle: "I repeat, black ladies and gentlemahn, the time has come for ahction! I, Ras the Destroyer, repeat, the *time has come!*" (p. 366). Having induced the crowd to erupt, Ras now wants to kill the Invisible Man, who has to escape. He tries to get back to Mary's, where he knows he can find refuge, and as he runs, the truth suddenly dawns on him:

If only I could turn around and drop my arms and say, "Look, men, give me a break, we're all black folks together . . . Nobody cares." Though now I knew *we* cared, they at last cared enough to act—so I thought. If only I could say, "Look, they've played another trick on us, the same old trick with new

variations—let's stop running and respect and love one another . . . " If only—
(p. 423)

But it is too late. "To Mary . . . to Mary" is his desperate hope, but
he never reaches her house. The apocalyptic cycle cannot be retracted,
and he must face the end. He manages to run away from Ras, but he
cannot escape his *real* destiny. Two white men try to kill him, and he
falls down a manhole from which he may never emerge again.

When the Invisible Man delivered the eulogy at the funeral of his
friend, Tod Clifton, he said: "That's the end in the beginning and
there's no encore" (p. 343). The same can now be said about himself.
In the previous cycles, destruction was followed by regeneration, but
this time there is no emerging from the coal cellar and starting all over
again. When the novel ends we realize that its overall cyclic structure
is not an upward spiral, but a vicious circle. Ellison's apocalypse is a
pessimistic one: it ends in destruction which leads not to regeneration
but to degeneration. The Invisible Man is left with his 1,369 light bulbs,
but they are no substitute for the reality, and he knows it.

The historical and political ramifications of Ellison's vision are perhaps too obvious to be discussed at length. His perspective was no less
conditioned by contemporary political developments than were Melville's or Twain's. The early 1950s were the years when the fight for
equal rights for the black people was only beginning. Ellison, however,
saw further: he was less concerned with the immediate victory for black
men than he was with the danger of his race being robbed of its identity.
In Ellison's book the black world goes through a series of apocalyptic
ends until it is finally destroyed, but the white world remains intact.
The mutual alienation of these two cultures seems to reach beyond
temporal conflicts and into eternal differentiation. Such dissimilarity is
not easy to overcome, and the years that have passed since the publication of *Invisible Man* had proven that the growth of racial awareness
helps increase the split rather than decrease it. If the Invisible Man ever
emerges from his underworld to participate in the creation of the new
earth, his voice, transmitted "on the lower frequencies," will be the
voice of his people, and only of his people.

NOTES

1. Ellin Horowitz, "The Rebirth of the Artist," in Richard Kostelanetz, ed.,
On Contemporary Literature, p. 330.

2. Ralph Ellison, *Invisible Man*, p. 3. Subsequent references in parentheses are to this edition.

3. Nathan A. Scott, Jr., ''Judgment Marked by a Cellar: The American Negro Writer and the Dialectic of Despair,'' in Harry J. Mooney, Jr., and Thomas F. Staley, eds., *The Shapeless God*, p. 167.

5

ROBERT COOVER:
APOCALYPSE AS IRONY

One of the factors that determines the character of literary apocalypse is the relative importance of either the destructive element or the promise of a happy new world. In the course of American literature the vision of the New World had been gradually disappearing, to the point where apocalypse came to signify little more than final and total destruction. There is indeed a message in the consistency with which the contemporary mind calls upon the symbolism of the Four Riders, the Whore of Babylon, and other disquieting figures of the Book of Revelation while at the same time disregarding the pastoral visions of the New World. To use but one example, the basically optimistic ending of Frank Coppola's film *Apocalypse Now* evoked a surprisingly critical reaction, caused primarily by our disbelief that anything can follow the End. Fictional ends are figures for our death, and while a happy ending is what we may secretly enjoy, its unwarranted optimism makes it incompatible with our experience.

The epilogue to Robert Coover's *The Origin of the Brunists*, appropriately entitled "Return," provides such a happy end: the book's likable protagonist, Justin Miller, who had previously "departed from this world,"[1] is miraculously brought back to life. While we may have hoped for his revival, we do feel a strange inconsistency here, as if death at the Mount of Redemption were the only acceptable end. Moreover, not only does Miller survive, but even his presumed death is accompanied by a scene of a woman giving birth to a child. Such suggestions of the cyclic pattern, which is not compatible with the structure of the Judaeo-Christian apocalypse, are a consequence of two dominant features of Coover's vision of the apocalypse. One is that his book is not so much apocalyptic as meta-apocalyptic, that is, it deals primarily not with the apocalypse itself but with its cult—chiliasm. In *The Sense of an Ending* Frank Kermode observes that "apocalypse can be disconfirmed without being discredited,"[2] and goes on to discuss various unfulfilled prophecies of the end of the world. Chiliasm can thus be considered a repetitive phenomenon which provides a basis for the cyclic structure of the book.

The other dominant feature of Coover's writings is the premeditated distance that he maintains between the traditional meaning of the ideas he deals with and his own treatment of them. The resulting effect of irony must be taken into account in all interpretations of his writings. Coover is thus aware of the nature of symbolic imagery traditionally employed in apocalyptic literature, and he constantly refers to these symbols. However, what the earlier "apocalyptic" writers treated in a straightforward manner, Coover approaches as a consciously designed game—with himself, with the readers, with the whole concept of symbolic representation. Such an attitude is, in a way, typical of all postmodern fiction. It is much more interested in its own matter than in the outside world, and has all but replaced the idea of mimesis with the concept of parody, or radical irony. While this approach is not common in apocalyptic writing, it is in contemporary American literature. Therefore it seems worthwhile to discuss Coover's works in order to find out how a postmodern author can play with the conventional chiliastic imagery to the point of turning it against itself and in effect nullifying its traditional intimidating aspect.

Coover's method can be perhaps best exemplified by his treatment of dates and numbers. The end-of-the-world prophecies have always been preoccupied with time and its measurement, with establishing the date when events such as the End are to occur. Throughout *The Origin of the Brunists* Coover is also very much concerned with giving exact dates. He keeps a precise count of how many days, weeks, or months pass between events, but in the process successfully conceals the crucial information: the year the End is to happen. Coover states repeatedly that Easter Sunday fell on April 11 that year, and the book obviously takes place after World War II, but the last time Easter Sunday fell on April 11 was in 1936, and the next time will not be before 1998. In effect, Coover not only places his book out of time, so to speak, but also provides a clue to his "reverse" treatment of chiliastic symbols: he uses them but at the same time disavows their basic pattern.

One of the main reasons why the Book of Revelation has inspired so many chiliastic prophecies is that it abounds in numbers.[3] Four and seven are used most consistently, but there are also other numbers which appear with significant frequency: twelve (names, tribes of Israel, courses of stones, gates), twenty-four (elders), hundred (and forty-four, as well as six hundred sixty-six), thousand (years), and so forth. Combined with continuous attempts at foreseeing the date of the world's end, this led to the creation of various arithmological cults based on counting words in a sentence or letters in a word, assigning numerical values to letters, and manipulating them more or less at will in order to arrive at a desired result. Coover's attitude toward this is again ironical, but the final effect is more than a simple rejection of such methods. His favorite procedure can be described as a three-tier construction. He presents some chiliastic belief, ridicules and apparently rejects it—and then goes on to include it in disguise somewhere else in the novel. Probably the best such example is provided by the description of the Brunists' emblem: "The dimensions of this pick/cross were numerologically determined: seven units each for the arms and head, twelve units for the post or handle...." Trained by the book's numerological messages, we quickly sum it up and arrive at the unquestionably symbolic figure of 33, only to find out that the rest of the sentence reads: " ... totaling thirty-three, the life in years of Christ not to mention an entire history of secondary meanings derived from important ancient writings" (p. 295). Double-crossed in this manner, we tend to disregard such obvious symbolism and may as a result overlook the fact that somewhere else in the book, in an apparently unrelated scene, somebody wins $33 on a TV show (p. 114), or that Bruno's mysterious abdominal scars spell out "LOF," which supposedly stands for either "love" or "laugh," (p. 300) but is never translated into its alphabet value in numbers, a procedure otherwise repeatedly and eagerly followed throughout the book. Having done this, we discover that with L equaling 12, O equaling 15, and F equaling 6, we also arrive at 33. The dimensions of the cross are "numerologically determined" as 7, 7, 7, and 12, and the obvious symbolism of both the components and the sum is ridiculed by the author, so what should we make of the fact that out of four chapters of the book itself, three consist of seven parts each, and one of twelve?

While the numerical symbols are essential for understanding Coover's method, it manifests itself through other symbolic constructions as well—always, however, retaining its equivocal character. The book begins with a coalmine disaster in which ninety-eight miners are believed to have perished. One of them, Giovanni Bruno, eventually survives, but due to a prolonged oxygen deficiency, his brain is permanently damaged. Prior to the catastrophe, another miner, who is also the preacher at the local Church of the Nazarene, Ely Collins, claimed to have seen a white bird in the mine. When his body is found, he has an unfinished letter with him which reads:

> DEAR CLARA AND ALL:
>> I dissobayed and I know I must Die.
>> Listen allways to the Holy Spirit in
>> your Harts Abide in Grace. We will
>> stand Together befor Our Lord the
>> 8th of   (p. 96)

In order to understand this scene properly, we must remember that in millennial speculations disasters or catastrophes are treated not so much as events in themselves but as signs, and earthquakes or underground explosions are among the "most definite" manifestations of God's anger. Ely Collins' vision provides a particularly rich source of apocalyptic predictions because the bird is an attribute of God and is related to Alpha and Omega (Yahveh was sometimes presented in the Bible as a bird). Moreover, both Christ and Satan have been symbolized by a bird, and white is the dominant color in the Revelation of St. John. The letter of the dying preacher provides, therefore, what many believe to be a message from God that the End is near. The reason why "the great majority of interpretations of Apocalypse assume that the End is pretty near," says Kermode, is that "the state of the world shows so clearly that the second coming is at hand, donec finiatur mundus corruptionis."[4] The community of West Condon is poor, there are no prospects, the mine disaster closes off the major source of employment—and the end of the world is in fact the only hope left for the people:

Or who can say why else this town's collective fate darkens so? The last of the area mines seems sure to close. The streets of the business sector grow desolate.... The winter is bitter and long. The families of ninety-seven dead coalminers huddle around old habits, their empty futures hovering like birds of prey.... Young people desert, breaking up families. A motel closes. The basketball team loses. A strange virus cripples half the community. The whole town seems to age overnight. Children grow rebellious. TV reception is often bad. A dance at the Eagles is cancelled. People die. The rate of harassment crimes rises. (p. 215)

The atmosphere of impending doom grows easily in such a combination of real and imaginary calamities, a true lack of future prospects, and tendentious interpretations of events:

Outwardly, the signs are few. Intimately, the message radiates. At a meeting, ministers are warned.... A priest, making a house visit, is bluntly turned away. An impeccable lawyer becomes irascible and unreliable. At an evening meeting of a Baptist youth group, "what if" questions are posed. Chiliastic warnings appear among the graffiti of boys' rest rooms.... A neighbor darkens her kitchen and sits by the window. Observes the furtive arrivals. The sinister preparations. The burning candles. The sheets over the windows. Hears the screams. (p. 220)

The new cult, of which Giovanni Bruno becomes the prophet, is soon joined not only by psychopaths, like the Nortons and Ralph Himebaugh, but also by Justin Miller, the editor of the West Condon *Chronicle*. He is by far the most complicated character in *The Origin of the Brunists*. His name is most readily associated with William Miller, the leader of the American Great Second Advent movement (known also as the Millerite movement), which achieved widespread popularity in the 1840s. He is generally known as "Tiger" Miller, but while this animal is one of Christ's emblems, Justin is soon declared an agent of the Powers of Darkness. Furthermore, Justin Miller's Christian name suggests St. Justin, a second-century Christian martyr who was trusted with spreading the Word, and Miller is given credit for securing worldwide recognition for the Brunists. *The Origin of the Brunists* opens with a quote from the Book of Revelation—"Write what you see in a book and send it to the Seven Churches" (Rev. 1:11)—and the analogy is clear: it was the duty of St. John to describe what he saw, and it is the duty of Miller to write about what *he* sees. But just as Miller did not create the faith, he cannot destroy it. During the Mount of Redemption ritual, "Miller notice[s] that the one thing that drew the crowd's attention from the hill were the instant copies of Polaroid cameras, exciting them even more than watching the real thing" (p. 407). He capitalizes on this knowledge, but at the same time realizes that all attempts to stop the Brunists must fail. Miller is a complex character cast in many contradictory roles, but on the whole he is a destroyer rather than a creator, a man who comes to West Condon with great promises but fails to help its inhabitants, a figure who is feared but usually not believed. In the apocalyptic system of symbols, he is the Antichrist. Yet he is also the only resurrected figure in the book, the only Christ figure—and there can be little doubt that this inconsistency is intentional, as is further proven by the character of Happy Bottom.

There are two women in Miller's life. One is the young and innocent Marcella, who becomes the Brunists' first victim and saint; the other is a beautiful nurse called Happy Bottom. She is not only sexually attractive and willing, but also unusually intelligent and witty. What makes her even more interesting is that the main object of her jokes is the Day of Judgement. Part IV, for instance, which begins with a quote from the Book of Revelation—"Come, gather for the great supper of God" (Rev. 19:17-18)—closes with another of her iconoclastic letters about the Last Judgement, the concluding sentence being an ironical: "Come and have breakfast." Critics have pointed to the "improbability" of her sobriquet[5] (we never learn her real name) without, however, noticing that it makes her initials read H. B. At least at one point in the novel the Book of Revelation is discussed and the Whore of Babylon is specifically mentioned: "The harlot is an image of a city, ... of a literal historic enemy, and, ultimately, of all the enemies of Christ" (p. 224). Not only is the word "harlot" used here: on another occasion, somebody spells the word *whore* as H-O-R-E. With Justin Miller as Antichrist, Happy Bottom can stand for the Whore of Babylon, though the symbolism is again ambiguous. She is also good-hearted, keeps helping people—a feature stressed by her profession—and, while she tries to win Miller over from Marcella, does not corrupt anybody.

The other woman in Miller's life, Marcella Bruno (sister of Giovanni), is certainly the most innocent member of the sect. She falls in love with Miller, a feeling he reciprocates; but while she wants to combine her newly discovered sexual desire with deep religious convictions, Miller's aim is to pull her away from the Brunists. Marcella remains in the cult, but as a result of her traumatic meeting with Justin she refuses all food and is subsequently killed on her way to the Mount of Redemption. Miller's destructive powers bring about the woman's death, but at the same time strengthen the movement as Marcella becomes its first martyr-saint. As if to stress her distance from the depraved, sections of the book that deal with her or her thoughts are always italicized: she is different not only from Miller, but also from other Brunists.

Finally, there is Giovanni Bruno. Apart from obvious associations with Giordano Bruno (Father Baglione instigates the excommunication procedure against Giovanni), his first name translates into English as John, which suggests an analogy with St. John. He also pronounces six cryptic "prophesies": *Hark ye to the White Bird; I am the One to Come; Coming of Light; Sunday Week, The tomb is its message; A circle of evenings; Gather on the Mount of Redemption*; and *Baptize Light*. With little effort they could all be linked not only with one another but also with the Book of Revelation. However, a more essential apocalyptic image is conveyed not through such similarities, but through the fact that the Brunists turn against Christianity, and toward paganism.

The history of the cult begins with Bruno's celebrated homecoming, which is scheduled for February 2; the day is chosen as an anniversary of the town's incorporation. At the same time it is Groundhog Day, with its folk tradition, and Candlemas, or the Presentation of the Child Jesus. Soon after the celebration the sect grows and acquires a strange mixture of beliefs. The Protestant minister, Abner Baxter, unsuccessfully rallies against it, and Father Baglione anathemizes Bruno, but the process cannot be stopped. Members of the group adopt new names (Marcella, for instance, is now called "Mana"); the Brunists object to the Catholic funeral of Bruno's father; and when they finally set their Creed, it is "based on the Seven Words of Giovanni Bruno and Saint Paul and the Revelation to John, and contain[s] wonderful new ideas about Mother Mary and Spiritual Communication and the God, not of Wrath or Love, but of Light" (p. 423).

This repudiation of Christianity—and partial rejection is in this case as effective as total renunciation—should be interpreted in light of the fact that apocalyptic prophecies are characterized by a predominant sense of history, by their inclination to use whatever the past has left us to foresee the future. The community of West Condon (the rest of the world being sometimes referred to as East Condon) has no present time: the explosion destroyed the last mine, and there is no other industry in the area. In despair, people turn to what they think has absolute value: numbers, messages sent by "other aspects," hidden meanings of Biblical texts. These, however, are not reliable either. They are frequently falsified, altered, and variously distorted. So, in a sense, is

The Origin of the Brunists itself, with its misleading clues, possibilities of different and conflicting interpretations of seemingly obvious symbols, and a happy end which is so disappointing. In one of the most improbable, and therefore most conspicuous, passages, Vince Bonali, a simple miner, says: "History is like a big goddamn sea . . . and here we are, bobbing around on it, a buncha poor bastards who can't swim, seasick, lost, unable to see past the next goddamn wave, not knowing where the hell it's taking us if it takes us anywhere at all" (p. 330). "Such are history's documents!" (p. 99), Miller adds derisively, but even if history's documents are indeed distorted, it does not follow that faith alone can teach us anything, or "take us anywhere."

The Origin of the Brunists seems to be a more intricate book than criticism of it has so far allowed, yet its complexity is self-destructive. Wherever we turn, we encounter new numbers, new symbols, clues, paths, which are designed to discredit and parody one another. Finally, we have to quit explaining "signs" for fear of becoming chiliasts ourselves, and double-crossed ones at that. Robert Coover uses apocalyptic imagery in order to question its foundations. His novel proves that skillful manipulation of signs and symbols can in fact produce the illusion of substance behind them, even if there is no "real" message to convey.

The subject-matter of Coover's next novel, *The Universal Baseball Association*, is again related to the apocalypse. The book is an attempt at presenting a traditional apocalyptic destruction-rebirth concept, and while its general framework is to some extent ironical, *The Universal Baseball Association* is not as permeated with the sense of parody as *The Origin of the Brunists*. The main figure of this book, J. Henry Waugh, is an accountant who, over a period of many years, has developed his hobby of game-playing into an essential part of his life. Having tried and discarded numerous games, he finally designs his own one, based on the rules of baseball. He proceeds to create a whole "league" of eight teams with players, umpires, officials, and reporters, and makes them go through entire seasons of tournaments. The game is played with dice and numerous charts, which not only decide the events on the field, but can also bring such occurrences as injuries, riots—or even players' deaths. Step by step, this new world encroaches on Henry's "real" life. It becomes his true reality, which he constantly recreates and develops with every throw of the dice.

The basic premise of *The Universal Baseball Association* is the concept of exhausted possibilities. The world of the Association is based on tossing three dice, which can render various combinations of digits. Some of them lead to another throw of the dice, or even two, but the number of arrangements is finite. When the last pattern is reached, the world, together with its god, can either start repeating itself or pass to a new "aspect." Three dice can form fifty-six different combinations and when the action takes place, the final, fifty-sixth variation is being reached on various levels. Henry "saw two time lines crossing in space at a point marked '56'. Was it the vital moment?"[6] Obviously, this is the crucial moment: J. Henry Waugh is himself fifty-six years old, his Association goes through its fifty-sixth season, the league's most celebrated hero, Brock Rutherford, is also fifty-six. The figure itself has a symbolic meaning: five stands for Christ and his church, while six is the number of imperfection; also, fifty is the number of the Holy Ghost, and six is that of the Beast of the Apocalypse. Something momentous is bound to happen. When it does, the old world is destroyed and a new one appears, thus following the pattern of the apocalypse. It is almost redundant to add that the process takes place between chapters 7 and 8 (7 times 8 equals 56 again). Coover, a perfect god, leaves nothing to chance.

It is therefore during this final, fifty-sixth year that the battle between good and evil takes place. In the game between the Knickerbockers and the Pioneers, baseball's rising star, Damon Rutherford, faces another young pitcher, Jock Casey. Damon Rutherford is a rookie player, but he already knows everything about baseball: he has just pitched a perfect game, and is but one inning short of establishing a world record of scoreless innings. He is also handsome, cool, and elegant, and quickly becomes everybody's idol. He seems to be the embodiment of all that is good, just, and perfect. Moreover, the relationship between Henry, the god of the book's universe, and the young Rutherford is in many ways a father-son relationship. Henry is emotionally attached to the boy, whose sudden death he mourns as if he were mourning the death of his real son. He fortifies the impression that Rutherford is the son of god by blending his death with the death of one Jim Creighton, whose initials, J. C., suggest an analogy with Jesus Christ. This is, however, where we again face Coover's confusing symbolism. Rutherford's first name is Damon, and lest we miss the point, someone says in the book: "Was it not thou that didst cut Rutherford in pieces, that didst deck the daemon?" (p. 232). Rutherford is the god's son, but he is also

Antichrist, who can destroy the universe of *The Universal Baseball Association*. To confound the symbolism even further, Rutherford's opponent is another rookie pitcher, who is determined to win the game, even though he has to play against the crowd, and who in the process kills "god's son," but whose name is Jock Casey, which makes his initials also read J. C.

As the fateful game begins, Henry feels the impending danger and wants to save his favorite player, but he realizes that he cannot interfere with the events determined by the dice without destroying the world he has created:

Oh, sure, he was free to throw away the dice, run the game by whim, but then what would be the point of it? . . . Even though he'd set his own rules, his own limits, and though he could change them whenever he wished, nevertheless he and his players were committed to the turns of the mindless and unpredictable—one might even say, irresponsible—dice. That was how it was. He had to accept it, or quit the game altogether. (p. 40)

He throws two triple ones, and a third such throw would mean the death of Rutherford. There is only one chance in fifty-six for this to happen, but this is the fifty-sixth year, the year of final events, and Henry realizes that he cannot throw anything but a triple one. He (or perhaps *his* creator, Robert Coover) tries to falsify the odds by saying that "there was only one chance in 216 that he'd throw a triple one," (p. 70) but that does not help, and Henry's third consecutive toss of triple ones announces Rutherford's death.

Henry is crushed, but in the following game he makes sure that Rutherford's "killer" is also killed. This time, however, he does not trust to chance. He violates his own rules by arranging the dice instead of throwing them. He exercises his power over the world he has brought into existence and avenges the death of his favorite player. In apocalyptic terms we could interpret this pattern as a temporal victory of Antichrist, who is then brought down by God. What Henry disregards is that the god is also bound by the rules he has created; if he breaks them, his world cannot survive in its present shape. When Henry violates this law, his universe is destroyed and a new structure is created in its place. The final, eighth chapter of the book (eight being a symbol of regeneration or a new beginning) is devoted to the description of this new reality.

Coover seems to combine here two end-of-the-world traditions. On the one hand, the destruction of the world is followed by the creation of a new world, according to the Judaeo-Christian pattern of the linear apocalypse. At the same time, the new world does not appear to be any better or happier than the old one. Even more important, its main ceremony is a periodic re-enactment of the events that brought the "old world" down. The actual cataclysm is not repeated, but there is constant fear that the pattern of the cyclic destruction and rebirth of the world will be followed and that the catastrophe will occur again:

"No, wait, Hardy, I'm not joking. Maybe . . . maybe, Hardy, they're really gonna kill you out there today!"
" . . . Bullshit, Skeeter. The old-timers just build it up to give the rookies a little scare each year. They'd have to be crazy to——" He's sorry the minute he's said it. (p. 227)

In view of this mixed symbolism, can we find a consistent pattern in the book, a central principle that brings together its conflicting assumptions? In a seemingly minor scene Henry talks to his landlord's son and tries on him the title for the history of the Association:

"The UBA in the balance—how does that sound to you, Benny?"
"Is it a riddle, Mr. Waugh? I'm not very good at riddles."
"Ha, ha! Yes, that's what it is! A riddle! You hit it on the head!" (pp. 212-213)

In all likelihood, there is indeed a riddle in the title, and possibly one that sets the whole book in the proper perspective. The Association is "in the balance" because the process of creating this new reality is not yet completed, or because the word *balance* suggests a balance sheet (Henry Waugh is an accountant). But it is also "unbalanced" because it does not have a consistent moral system, because Antichrist is god's son, and because it is God who kills Christ. If notions such as sin, virtue, the Last Judgement, the New World are to have any meaning at all, it is necessary to establish a framework of moral values. Apocalypse has no meaning in a world where there is no clear distinction between good and evil, and Henry's Association is such a world. He creates his players, names them, makes them participate in the game, and ultimately kills them, but fails to provide them with a higher reason for their existence. "God does not play dice with the Universe," Albert Einstein was fond of saying, and *The Universal Baseball Association* shows that a world based on probability but devoid of deeper principles will never be a balanced one.

Coover's next novel, *The Public Burning*, has a much clearer moral frame. The opposition between good and evil constitutes the main theme of the book. Yet the novel also uses irony, and its main ironic device consists in reversing the value system. The mean and vengeful are referred to as Forces of Light, while the innocent victims are said to represent the Powers of Darkness. However, in order to understand the book's message we have to refer its plot to the outside reality. Only after the novel's main characters are compared with the historical Rosenbergs can we fully appreciate Coover's irony and arrive at a correct moral judgement.

Apocalypse consists not only of such imitable elements as the fight between Christ and Antichrist, Armageddon, and the process of rebirth, but first of all of the "sense of the end." In order to achieve the effect of impending apocalypse, a writer must be able to convey to his readers the sense of the immediacy of destruction which results from associating the danger with the reader's experience. Melville's readers may never have been at sea, and Ellison's might never have lived in Harlem, yet the worlds of *Moby Dick* and *Invisible Man* correspond to the readers' reality through their unmistakably mimetic quality and a recognizable system of values. The same cannot be said of *The Universal Baseball Association*, with its self-referential structure, and a value system that is violated by the creator.

NOTES

1. Robert Coover, *The Origin of the Brunists*, p. 410. Subsequent references in parentheses are to this edition.

2. Frank Kermode, *The Sense of an Ending*, p. 8.

3. Cf. Leon Morris, *Apocalyptic*, p. 37.

4. Kermode, *The Sense of an Ending*, p. 8.

5. Leo J. Hertzel, "What's Wrong with the Christians," p. 18.

6. Robert Coover, *The Universal Baseball Association, Inc., J. Henry Waugh, Prop.*, p. 50. Subsequent references in parentheses are to this edition.

6

FROM RUDOLF CLAUSIUS TO HERMAN MELVILLE: ENTROPY AS A LITERARY CONCEPT

When the great scientific revolution of the late nineteenth century shattered the foundations of Newtonian physics, based on certainty and the unfailing cause-and-effect chain, one of its indirect results was a drastic change in man's attitude toward his universe. His world was no longer reliable and safe. Statistical probability replaced neat causal relations, and other similarly disconcerting ideas abounded: neither Freud's discoveries in psychology nor Darwin's theory of evolution helped restore man's faith in nature. When adapted to the needs of literature, however, these theories had a stimulating effect. They accounted for the birth of naturalism, the creation of stream-of-consciousness techniques, and other developments in twentieth-century prose and poetry. One such concept, which originated in science and subsequently entered literature, was entropy. The notion was introduced by Rudolf Clausius in 1852, and in terms other than strictly physical, it is defined as "the ultimate state reached in the degradation of the matter and energy of the universe: state of inert uniformity of component elements: absence of form, pattern, hierarchy, or differentiation"; "the irreversible tendency of a system including the universe, toward increasing disorder and inertness; also, the final state predictable from this tendency"; or a "hypothesized tendency toward uniform inertness, esp. of the universe."[1]

Entropy was introduced to literature through history, and particularly through Henry Adams' theory of historical development. Adams described the Second Law of Thermodynamics, the law of entropy, by saying that "the higher powers of energy tended always to fall lower, and that this process had no known limit."[2] He went on to say that "all nature's energies were slowly converting themselves into heat and vanishing in space, until, at the last, nothing would be left except a dead ocean of energy at its lowest possible level . . . incapable of doing any work whatever" (p. 145).

In the process of translating a physical term into a historiographical one, Adams established two crucial principles which greatly contributed to the term's subsequent popularity in twentieth-century American literature. First, he found it possible to treat what he called Vital Energy, and the form of it called Social Energy, in the same way as any other type of energy, and thus to submit them to the processes described by the Second Law of Thermodynamics: "The law of Entropy imposes a servitude on all energies, including the mental" (p. 251). Then, while deploring some vulgar interpretations it might entail, Adams portrayed society as composed of separate (and therefore closed) groups. This last statement is particularly important for the application of the concept of entropy to literature. For entropy to occur at all, there must exist a closed system; otherwise, an outside supply of energy could balance its losses and stop the process. On the other hand, a man cannot usually be treated as a closed system: "We, as human beings, are not isolated systems. We take in food, which generates energy, from the outside, and . . . we take in information through our sense organs."[3]

Literary critics, aware of the discrepancy, have attempted to reconcile it in various ways. Tony Tanner, for instance, argued that many contemporary American novels "concentrate on people who precisely *are* turning themselves into 'isolated systems' . . . they take in a decreasing amount of information, sensory data, even food."[4] While this is true of some characters (Slothrop in Pynchon's *Gravity's Rainbow* is a very good case in point), the disintegrating influence of entropy can also be seen when such processes either do not occur at all, or are of very little importance (for instance, in *The Crying of Lot 49*). If, however, we take into consideration not only the Vital Energy of individual characters, but also the Social Energy of particular (and, according to Adams, separate) groups, we may discuss the entropic process in a given book even if particular characters are left unaffected by it.

As helpful and inspiring as Adams' assumptions were, they nonetheless referred basically to the physical concept of energy, and their application to history produced a possibly exaggerated picture of an impending catastrophe. While some novelists, such as Nathanael West and, to some degree, F. Scott Fitzgerald, used this "black" imagery in their works, such a necessarily bleak vision could not be universally accepted, and entropy did not gain much ground in literature. The crucial change occurred when Norbert Wiener applied the law of entropy to the theory of information. In *The Human Use of Human Beings*, he claimed that "it is possible to treat sets of messages as having an entropy like sets of states of the external world" (p. 21). Literature could now use the theme with comparative ease. Rather than translating physical terms into literary ones, writers understood that the very matter of fiction, communication among people, was also influenced by entropy, and that it was possible to present the process in art without necessarily resorting to scientific imagery. Moreover, while Adams concluded "that life had no meaning; the quest ended in a sheer, blank void from which there was no way of escape,"[5] Wiener offered a way out. Saying that "it is possible to interpret the information carried by a message as essentially the negative of its entropy ... that is, the more probable the message, the less information it gives" (p. 21), he almost set the course for what we frequently describe as "experimental" literature. If the less probable message counters entropy more effectively, then searching for new ways of expression is a dynamic process which may in fact save literature from languishing.

American literature of the last twenty years has indeed accepted this assumption. Postmodern fiction uses the theme of entropy more than ever (and anywhere) before, but develops at the same time new techniques and forms that help contain the process. There is, however, a latent danger in this approach. It would follow from what has been said that the most improbable messages, namely those composed of words haphazardly put together, could most effectively counter entropy and provide the greatest amount of information. Such works of literature have in fact been created, but common sense tells us that they have neither decreased the level of entropy nor offered much information. Actually, the opposite seems true: they tend to lower communication levels, and render the message meaningless. Does this mean that the whole relation suggested by Wiener proves false when brought to its logical consequence? It does not, and the paradox can be solved by considering the other source of entropy as well: disorder.

In his lecture on "The Atomic Theory of Matter," the physicist Max Planck said that it is the hypothesis of elementary disorder, which forms the real kernel of the principle of increase of entropy and, therefore the preliminary condition for the existence of entropy. Without elementary disorder there is neither entropy nor irreversible process.[6]

Discussing the relationship between entropy and art, Rudolf Arnheim added that

the increase of entropy is due to two quite different kinds of effect; on the one hand, a striving toward simplicity, which will promote orderliness and the lowering of the level of order, and, on the other hand, disorderly destruction.[7]

In their final effect these two tendencies amount to the same thing: one would feel equally lost in a totally chaotic environment, where no two elements are in an orderly relation with each other, and in an environment consisting only of uniform elements, where the surplus of orderliness would render all differentiation impossible.

In order to avoid entropy, a writer must therefore walk a narrow path between the danger of producing probable messages of low informational value (such as, for example, new versions of old themes, written in a conventional manner), and the risk of turning out incomprehensible bodies of words that would seem disorderly to the reader. The reader, and not only the author, must be taken into consideration as a factor. Physical entropy occurs in the world around us whether we notice it or not; it has been in progress ever since the universe was created, even though the process was discovered and named only a century ago. Informational entropy, on the other hand, depends not so much on the nature of the message as on the conditions of its transmisssion: who sends it to whom and under what circumstances. "Clichés," says Wiener, "are less illuminating than great poems," but this certainly is not true for someone who for the first time learns that "an apple a day keeps the doctor away," and who is later introduced, unprepared, to T. S. Eliot's *The Waste Land*. In order to discuss entropy in literature, a certain level of reader preparedness must therefore be assumed.

Finally, one must remember that physical entropy is not a force, but the numerical expression of a process. In literature, however, it is frequently treated as a force or as a conspiracy, a plot designed by a mysterious *Them*. Such attribution of "substance" to entropy was perhaps unavoidable when the notion moved from science to the arts, but we should nonetheless be aware of its nature, and remember that while the Manichean interpretation of entropy may seem more convincing than the Augustinian one,[8] there is no reason to reverse the procedure and look for an "evil force" every time entropy appears in a work of literature.

One more factor should be considered before passing to analyses of particular works. The notion of entropy has permeated American fiction to a very high degree, yet its influence is considerably weaker in the literature of other countries. While such phenomena can rarely be understood in full, and although our concern here is limited to American literature, some explanation of the unequal popularity of the idea can help us understand the role of entropic imagery in the course of American fiction.

Probably the most "literary" explanation is connected with the duration and influence of another American literary phenomenon, naturalism. While it was never the only mode of expression acceptable at a given time, naturalism can easily be found in almost all American fiction written through the 1940s, which is not the case anywhere else. This long-lasting fascination, related to an interest in the laws and processes of nature, made American writers more receptive to notions related to the natural sciences. Moreover, basic assumptions of naturalism can be traced back to Darwin's theory of evolution, which is connected in a specific manner with the concept of entropy.

Darwin's theory assumed that species evolved, developed, and changed, but it did not concern itself with the question of energy, presumably required for such processes. Henry Adams argued that while Darwin did not address the problem directly, his reasoning contradicted the First Law of Thermodynamics (that the sum of energy is constant) in assuming that "Vital Energy could be added, and raised indefinitely in potential, without the smallest apparent compensation" (p. 154). Even though Adams' argument can be disputed (on the grounds that evolution, as understood by Darwin if not by all of his followers, does not necessarily imply advancement that would require an additional supply of energy), there is no doubt that Darwin's theory stands in direct opposition to the Second Law of Thermodynamics. Vital processes can either evolve into more perfect forms, or be subjected to the process of energy decrease and therefore proceed only toward death. These two options contradict each other directly and are thus dialectically connected: a prolonged interest in one keeps the other potentially alive. As naturalism began to lose its position in American literature, one of the consequences was an increased interest in entropy. Darwin's theory was certainly more popular in America for almost a century, possibly because its assumptions corresponded to some basic American myths of social advancement and achievement. To substitute for it the Second Law was to vouch for a basically pessimistic *Weltanschauung*, to admit that while we can achieve temporary and local improvement, disintegration and decay cannot be escaped. (Characteristically, Henry Adams was an outspoken advocate of entropy in the later part of his life, when he was so obviously disillusioned with the world.)

Another important factor that helped elevate entropy to its dominant position in the American consciousness and in American literature in the second half of the century was a general knowledge of, and fascination with, science, markedly higher than in Europe. When in 1959 C. P. Snow presented his famous Rede Lecture at Cambridge University, in which he claimed that Western society had not only split into two polarized groups—literary intellectuals and scientists—but also—and more important—that each group was virtually ignorant of the other's achievements, he quoted the Second Law of Thermodynamics as an example of "basic science" that a literary man should know, but does not. Snow's remarks seem, however, to have been oriented toward Europe: Tony Tanner quotes John Hollander to the effect that all American schoolboys know this particular bit of "science" (p. 141). There is indeed little doubt that mid-twentieth century American society is science-oriented and probably more receptive to such notions than other societies. The publication of Norbert Wiener's *The Human Use of Human Beings* also contributed to this general awareness of scientific achievements. The book, which laid down the foundations of cybernetics, appeared in 1950, and while its treatment of entropy was rather limited, the second edition of 1954 provides probably the best introduction to the general implications of the notion. The book has since become, in Tanner's words, "something of a modern American classic and may well have been read by many of the [contemporary] writers" (p. 144).

Finally, there is the question of living conditions, and the relationship between the social situation and the general receptiveness to certain notions or ideas. It is worthwhile to quote in this context Claude Lévi-Strauss, who says in *Tristes Tropiques* that "urbanization and agriculture are themselves instruments intended to create inertia, at a rate and in a proportion infinitely higher than the amount of organization they involve''[9] (inertia being here a synonym for entropy, which Lévi-Strauss explains later on). Agriculture and stereotypical urbanization are at their highest in the United States and in many respects conditions in this country are indeed particularly conducive to entropic visions of the kind perhaps best exemplified by Stanley Elkin's *The Franchiser*.

It is hard to assess which of these reasons has been most instrumental in making entropy an important factor in contemporary American fiction. Only some of them are literary, while others are sociological, and they are not always compatible. The elevation of entropy to the position of a controlling metaphor in contemporary prose was certainly facilitated by the continuing interest in apocalypse in American culture. The fear of universal annihilation remains an essential factor in determining the state of the American national consciousness, regardless of whether the destruction is to be brought about by fire or ice.

Entropic, or entropy-related, concepts can be found in literature long before the notion was formulated by scientists, and Pope's *Dunciad* is frequently cited as an example. Such works were, however, neither numerous nor typical, and the real career of the concept (if not yet of the term itself) begins in the middle of nineteenth century. The idea of *Zeitgeist* is probably one of the most elusive and difficult to pin down, but we may consider the following concurrence in time. The Second Law of Thermodynamics was enunciated by Clausius in a paper delivered in Berlin in 1850, and the term *entropy* was proposed two years later. Almost simultaneously, in 1853, Charles Dickens' *Bleak House* dramatized the concept of the gradual but inescapable decay and dissolution of the physical world—and in the same year Herman Melville wrote *Bartleby the Scrivener*. It is most unlikely that either Dickens or Melville was familiar with Clausius' work, yet the same basic philosophical assumption was shared by all three, and it seems worthwhile to see just how closely Melville's vision corresponded to what we now recognize as the literary version of entropic concepts.

The unnamed narrator of *Bartleby the Scrivener* (''I am a rather elderly man'') is a lawyer who employs in his office an unusual motley of copyists. One, called Turkey, could work efficiently only until noon; for the rest of the day ''not only would he be reckless, and sadly given to making blots . . . but, some days, he went further, and was rather noisy.''[10] Nippers, another scrivener, displayed "irritability and consequent nervousness . . . in the morning, while in the afternoon he was comparatively mild'' (p. 9). The third employee, Ginger Nut, was only twelve years old, and his main duty was to provide the other two with ginger-nut cakes. The law office seems to be self-sufficient; the "stillness of the chambers" is stressed, and all descriptions center on the four people working together from early morning till late afternoon. Melville succeeds thus in creating what we can call an effect of the closed system, which is strengthened with another idea entailed by the entropic situation—equilibrium. Equilibrium is one of the most fundamental notions in the theory of entropy, without which the process need not increase, and Melville achieves a similar effect by balancing Turkey's and Nipper's temperaments: "Their fits relieved each other, like guards. When Nipper's was on, Turkey's was off; and *vice versa*" (p. 9).

When the story begins, the narrator has just received a Master in Chancery's office and needs another scrivener. Bartleby answers the advertisement and is hired. His initial description is already suggestive—the new employee is not only "pallidly neat" and "incurably forlorn," but first of all makes the impression of a "motionless man." While an outside intrusion usually destroys a closed system, it does not in this case: Bartleby is assigned to a place where he can be isolated from the other scriveners. The new clerk not only does not destroy the existing balance but in fact makes the most of it. While everybody else goes home after work, Bartleby is discovered to be living in the office and never leaving it: Melville resorts to the use of italics to stress that "*he was always there.*" The narrator soon discovers that the young scrivener never eats dinner—in fact, he eats nothing but ginger-nuts. Bartleby also refuses to follow or even receive any instructions from anybody and we are again reminded of Norbert Wiener's remark that human beings do not usually succumb to entropy because "we take in food and information." Bartleby does not, and as a result becomes himself a closed system, cut off from outside supplies and therefore a potential victim of entropy. He keeps refusing to do anything ("I would prefer not to") to the point of complete withdrawal, and his obstinacy makes the narrator change offices. Bartleby does not move and must be forced out of the premises. By that time, however, he has established his own closed system and the change of environment makes no discernible difference. He is taken to jail, where he keeps refusing to eat or talk and dies quietly "huddled at the base of the wall . . . wasted" (p. 42).

From the moment of his arrival at the office, Bartleby distinguishes himself by his mechanical behavior. He not only "[writes] on silently, palely, mechanically," but all his movements and reactions are similarly inanimate. While his employer senses that Bartleby's marasmus is not caused by laziness but by some other mysterious cause, he cannot name it. The victim seems to know the cause but does not care to explain it:

> "Why, how now? What next?" exclaimed I, "do no more writing?"
> "No more."
> "And what is the reason?"
> "Do you not see the reason for your-self?" he indifferently replied.
> (p. 26)

Just as the "elementary disorder" is the source of the entropic process which subsequently expands, Bartleby's behavior begins to influence other people. They are annoyed with him, but also seem to fall under his spell, and even begin to use his favorite expressions. His employer realizes that Bartleby "had already and seriously affected [him] in a mental way" (p. 25), and resorts to aimless trips around New York to avoid Bartleby (which is also how Pynchon's Benny Profane and Updike's Harry Angstrom react to similar anxieties). Changing offices, breaking away from the "closed system" in which he finds himself, is in fact the only way to save himself and others from destruction and decay, but even so Bartleby may have already influenced those around him.

The realistic tradition required Melville to provide some "rationale" for Bartleby's behavior. It turns out, therefore, that the scrivener used to be a clerk in the Dead Letter Office, where he supposedly acquired his "style." Melville, however, is quick to point out a similarity, perhaps more easily discernible to us than to his contemporaries: "Dead letters! does it not sound like dead men?" (p. 43), and the concept of entropy is most readily connected with the idea of death—be it of a system, of people, or of the universe. "Ah, Bartleby! Ah, humanity!" is the story's closing line, and one cannot miss the point that it is we, the readers, who will all fall prey to entropy.

Melville's fable stands alone among earlier American fiction in its presentation of entropic ideas. It was not until the turn of the century that Henry Adams made the term, and the concept behind it, more widely known. Even so, the first decades of the twentieth century were more receptive to various apocalyptic visions than to entropic ones. "Apocalyptic utopias," such as Ignatius Donnelly's *Caesar's Column*, were quite popular, as were the "racial apocalypses" of Thomas Dixon. The Spanish-American War, the assassination of President McKinley, impending World War I, would all encourage precisely such apocalyptic visions, rather than a relatively "quiet," entropic concept of a slowly dying world. The same, of course, was true of the years immediately following the war.

Another factor that accounted for the limited popularity of entropy was the requirements of realistic fiction which, despite early efforts by Faulkner and, to some extent, Dos Passos, dominated the American literary scene. Apocalyptic art, deeply rooted in Western culture and tradition, can be reconciled with the principles of realism, even if its highly symbolic ways contradict some of realism's more stringent rules. Entropy, on the other hand, was not so much a mode, or style, as a basically different way of perceiving one's *raison d'être*, teleology, and the meaning of the world around us—none of which could be expressed without violating basic principles of realism. This is not to say that the concept was totally ignored; traces of it may be found, for instance, in F. Scott Fitzgerald's *The Great Gatsby*. In literatures other than American, the best-known name is that of Yevgeny Zamyatin, whose *We* (1920), together with his theoretical essays, stands out as an early attempt at putting the concept of entropy to work in the sphere of social behavior. On the whole, however, entropy's time had not yet come; the only important exception in American literature seems to be the work of Nathanael West.

West's *A Cool Million* is basically a satire aimed at the American Dream and related myths, but the story of Lemuel Pitkin's body has obvious entropic overtones. In the course of events he has his teeth substituted for by artificial plates, his eye replaced with glass, and his leg removed and substituted for with a wooden prosthesis. Without overplaying the similarity, we can point out that, upon her death, Pynchon's *V.* is also discovered to be composed largely of artificial members. Both characters can thus be said to exemplify an interpretation according to which entropy in human beings means gradual reduction from the animate to the inanimate, which is a fairly frequent symbolic representation of the process.

The theme of gradual but inescapable death also lies at the center of West's *The Day of the Locust*. Tod Hackett, an aspiring painter, comes to realize that most of Los Angeles' inhabitants "had come to California to die."[11] He lives in the closed, self-sufficient, but at the same time self-destructive system of Hollywood, and perceives it as a gigantic trash pile, reminiscent of works by the Italian "painters of Decay and Mystery":

In the center of the field was a gigantic pile of sets, flats and props. . . . And the dump grew continually, for there wasn't a dream afloat somewhere which wouldn't sooner or later turn up on it. (p. 140)

This destruction and eventual dumping of human beings is best seen in the example of Homer Simpson, a middle-aged Midwesterner. In an almost archetypal entropic description his body begins to fail:

Every part was awake but his hands. They still slept. . . . They demanded special attention. . . . When he had been a child, he used to stick pins into them and once had even thrust them into a fire. Now he used only cold water. (p. 48)

The freezing spreads, and when destruction comes, it is a result of both Homer's lack of survival instinct and the crowd's inertia. Tod tries to oppose the catastrophe by concentrating mentally on his apocalyptic painting, titled "The Burning of Los Angeles," but he fails to impose his vision upon the reality. Inertia and chaos prevail, people are crushed to death, and Homer is the symbolic victim who gives up struggling and is run over by the crowd.

Obviously, not all chaos and disorder are necessarily entropic, but West's familiarity with the notion, and possibly his entropic intentions, are proven by his earlier novel, *Miss Lonelyhearts*. Miss Lonelyhearts' destruction is a result of his own "insane sensitiveness to order" and a desire to improve the world by imposing a better structure on it. He offers Christian love as an alternative, but realizes that nothing can successfully counter the entropic chaos inherent in the world around us:

He sat in the window thinking. Man has tropism for order. Keys in one pocket, change in another. Mandolins are tuned G D A E. The physical world has a tropism for disorder, entropy. Man against Nature . . . the battle of the centuries. Keys yearn to mix with change. Mandolins strive to get out of tune. Every order has within it the germ of destruction.[12]

When West died tragically in 1940, he was a little-known writer, yet today his novels are widely recognized as modern American classics. West's preoccupation with the entropic vision was understandably out of tune with the America of his time, which was gathering strength to come out of the Great Depression. His readers could not accept a view as gloomy and devoid of hope as West's. The principle of entropy was anathema because it seemed to express the basic idea of the Crisis: uncontrollable, irreversible, and destructive decay. The rediscovery of West coincided with the rediscovery by American writers of entropy in an era that seems more resigned to the inevitability of its implications. It would be difficult, and indeed superfluous, to establish that *Bartleby the Scrivener* or West's novels contributed directly to the theme's popularity in contemporary writing, but they certainly constitute an important historical source of inspiration, without which the writings of Thomas Pynchon, Susan Sontag, or John Updike might not have been received with such readiness and understanding.

NOTES

1. Cf. *Webster's Third New International Dictionary; American Standard College Dictionary*; and *The Random House Dictionary*.
2. Henry Adams, ''A Letter to American Teachers of History,'' in *The Degradation of the Democratic Dogma*, p. 141. Subsequent references in parentheses are to this edition.
3. Norbert Wiener, *The Human Use of Human Beings*, p. 28. Subsequent references in parentheses are to this edition.
4. Tony Tanner, *City of Words*, p. 146. Subsequent references in parentheses are to this edition.
5. George Hochfield, *Henry Adams*, p. 139.
6. Max Planck, *Eight Lectures on Theoretical Physics*, pp. 50-51.
7. Rudolf Arnheim, *Entropy and Art: An Essay on Disorder and Order*, p. 52.
8. For an interesting discussion of the problem see Wiener, *Human Beings*, pp. 34-36, 190-91.
9. Claude Lévi-Strauss, *Tristes Tropiques*, p. 413.

10. Herman Melville, *Bartleby the Scrivener*, p. 6. Subsequent references in parentheses are to this edition.

11. Nathanael West, *The Day of the Locust*, p. 5. Subsequent references in parentheses are to this edition.

12. Nathanael West, *Miss Lonelyhearts*, pp. 115-16.

7

THOMAS PYNCHON, OR,
THE INEVITABILITY
OF DESTRUCTION

The main theme of Thomas Pynchon's early story entitled "Entropy" is that closed systems are subject to an irreversible and continuous process of thermodynamic or informational entropy. While numerous interpretations have dealt extensively with entropy's role in the story,[1] one element of it is particularly worth remembering. At the end of "Entropy," Callisto's girlfriend decides to break the window in order to terminate his obsession with maintaining the closed system. We could expect that this act would lead to Callisto's "universe" returning into the larger, "real" one and, consequently, would bring to an end the entropic process in the sealed-off apartment. While the world outside also undergoes a similar process, it proceeds at a different pace there, and the smaller system would receive an energy input which would decrease its entropy. Instead she

turned to face the man on the bed and waited with him until the moment of equilibrium was reached, when 37 degrees Fahrenheit should prevail both outside and inside, and forever, and the hovering, curious dominant of their separate lives should resolve into a tonic of darkness and the final absence of all motion.[2]

The smaller system will thus subdue the larger one as 37° (which is also body temperature measured in centigrade) gradually prevails throughout the world and becomes its final temperature.

In a way this may be understood as the main principle of Pynchon's interpretation of entropy. It is not the only motif in his fiction, in some cases not even the most evident one. Yet, as Pynchon's worlds develop and follow one another, entropy gradually establishes itself as the controlling metaphor to which all others are submitted. The theme of this early story dominates the universe of each of Pynchon's three novels to date and has underscored the meaning of "Entropy."

Pynchon's early stories were not widely known, and when his first novel, *V.*, appeared in 1963, it was not immediately compared with "Entropy." However, the notion was so dominant in the book that *V.* was generally understood as a description of the entropic process. There is indeed no doubt that the novel evolves around such notions as decadence, decay, anarchy, and randomness. All these terms are either used explicitly in the book or very clearly implied, though entropy, which is their common denominator and the single power behind what happens in *V.*, is never mentioned by name.

In his penetrative essay on Pynchon, Tony Tanner stresses that the animate elements of *V.* turn into inanimate ones, that things acquire greater importance than people.[3] The most significant example of this is supposedly provided by *V.* herself: after she has died under the guise of the Bad Priest, she is discovered to be composed of mechanical components rather than of human parts. It seems, however, that Tanner's argument disregards an important distinction which concerns not only Pynchon's works, but the literary meaning of entropy in general. Not only can mechanisms be relatively sophisticated (and Pynchon's frequently are), but first of all the concept that seems more justifiable than "entropy" here is "objectification," which simply means that human beings are turned into things. While objects are as a rule less "alive" than beings, this alone is not enough to establish the presence of the entropic process.

Under certain circumstances, however, objectification can lead to entropy, particularly if the very quality of being human is involved. The most obvious such case results from von Trotha's extermination plan ("Vernichtungs Befehl"), which called for unconditional extermination of all Hereroes and Hottentots and was only later made more "lenient" through the establishment of forced labor camps:

And so, as you moved among them, you were forced to look at them as a collection: knowing from statistics that twelve to fifteen of them died per day, but eventually unable even to wonder which twelve to fifteen: in the dark they differed only in size, and that made it easier not to care as you once had.[4]

Such treatment of black slaves can still be described as simply another aspect of objectification, but only until it results in a change in the attitude of the other party, the German soldiers. They were forbidden to develop any emotion and were not allowed to treat their victims as human beings or establish any relation with them. As a consequence they were afflicted almost as much: the intentional depersonalization took its toll not only among the victims, but also among the oppressors:

If a season like the Great Rebellion ever came to him again, he feared, it could never be in that same personal, random array of picaresque acts . . . but rather with a logic that chilled the comfortable perversity of the heart, that substituted capability for character, deliberate scheme for political epiphany. (p. 273)

Only in this context can we fully see the significance of V. What matters is not so much her own reduction to the inanimate state as the fact that people who in one way or another are associated with her gradually become dehumanized. A small system again forces a larger one to accept its rules. In this sense V.'s influence is indeed entropic, as depersonalization can be considered equivalent to depriving objects of the diversity of physical qualities.

The effectiveness of V. is increased by the abundance of closed systems in the novel's reality. Flopp's siege party is the most obvious example of a self-sufficient closed system with no outside supply of any kind, and the Whole Sick Crew seems to be able to function regardless of the world around. Men-of-war, by definition self-enclosed, are the location of much of the novel's action, and the underground sewer system, in which Benny Profane and others hunt alligators, exists independently of the rest of the city. There is also Malta, which plays a crucial role in the book by being a self-contained island that shuns all contacts with the mainland, and Vheissu, about which little is known except for its impenetrability. Finally, V. herself is a closed system whose existence depends on how effectively she can frustrate other people's attempts at establishing contact. What Pynchon also implies is that such closed systems are attractive to outsiders, who keep trying to penetrate them. A large part of the book's plot centers around such attempts, with V. being the most coveted goal. The trap is that V.

induces the entropic process and thus brings destruction to all who approach her.

Her devastating influence is best exemplified by what happens to Herbert Stencil. Before he begins his search of V. he lives a free life, deprived of any particular purpose. The search organizes Stencil's life, but he soon realizes that the success of his efforts would signify the ultimate organization of his life and lead to his own destruction. To preserve his own identity, he purposefully rejects a chance to find out the secret of V.'s identity. Instead, he leaves Malta and goes to Stockholm in pursuit of one Mme. Viola, another meaningless impersonation of V.

Entropy, however, can mean not only fatal over-structuring but also fatal disorder—which in fact threatens to destroy another character closely related to V., Fausto Maijstral. His personal sense of search is connected with his sense of Malta's history and of the potentially dangerous influence of V. He realizes that while his persistence may result in uncovering the secret, it will unavoidably result in destruction, referred to as "decadence" but explained in terms unmistakably reminiscent of entropy, in itself one of the "laws of physics":

Decadence, decadence. What is it? Only a clear movement toward death or, preferably, non-humanity. As Fausto II and III, like their island, became more inanimate, they moved closer to the time when like any dead leaf or fragment of metal they'd be finally subject to the laws of physics. (p. 321)

By approaching V. too closely one runs a danger of dehumanization, and already the universe of *V.* is partly non-human. It is populated with humanoids like SHROUD and SHOCK, and Benny Profane dreams of an electronic woman that would cause no metaphysical problems:

Someday, please God, there would be an all-electronic woman. Maybe her name would be Violet. Any problems with her, you could look it up in the maintenance manual.... Remove and replace, was all. (p. 385)

While such a woman exists so far only in Profane's dreams, SHOCK and SHROUD are actually used by Anthroresearch Association test laboratories. Benny Profane endows them with a kind of consciousness and spends nights discussing various problems with them, which in turn provides justification for their classification as "Synthetic Human Objects.'' When SHROUD says, ''Me and SHOCK are what you and everybody will be someday'' (p. 286), there are enough concurrent developments in *V.* to make us believe that the prophecy may come true and that the entropic process will prevail. In *V.*, says Richard Patteson, ''technology, the instrument that man thinks can further his evolution to the superhuman, is really the death trap that hastens his reduction to the subhuman.''[5]

Does this mean that SHROUD (and, by extension, technology) conspires against man? *V.* seems to be full of mysterious plotters, manipulators, agents—but do they ''really'' exist or are they simply a product of the characters' imaginations? In other words, is the entropic process intensified by some malign power, or does it simply follow its own course, remaining in a way ''detached'' from the disintegrating world? It seems that the characters that inhabit the world of *V.* want to believe that such plots and schemes exist because shapeless entropic forces would be even more terrifying. Benny Profane personifies his fears in SHROUD and SHOCK, which quietly survive even the disaster that Benny partly causes. Stencil, who is much more sophisticated, constructs the figure of V., hoping that he will have to deal with intentional plots rather than with inescapable decay. Mondaugen looks for meaning in what seems to be a random series of atmospheric radio disturbances. He does it in an effort to avoid reality, which nonetheless catches up with him when Weissmann, an early follower of Hitler's concept of law and order, claims to have discovered that the ''sferics'' did convey a message. It supposedly consists of Mondaugen's own name and Wittgenstein's famous opening proposition: *Die Welt ist alles was der Fall ist.* As another character, Eigenvalue, puts it, ''This sort of arranging and rearranging was Decadence, but the exhaustion of all possible permutations and combinations was Death'' (p. 298).

The alternatives therefore seem severely limited: on the one hand decadence, decay, or disorder leading to entropy, and on the other death by exhaustion or by ultimate ordering, when no energy is available due to the disappearance of meaningful differences. No matter which course is chosen, it will ultimately lead to the entropic death: ''*V.* describes the thermodynamic process by which the world's entropy increases and by which the world's available energy declines.''[6] This in turn is combined with informational entropy, exemplified not only by Mondaugen's ''sferics,'' but also by the fact that some twenty languages are used in the book,[7] which results in confusion and a decrease of meaningful information being passed around and received with comprehension. In this context it may be worth repeating that the word *entropy* does not appear in the book at all, as if Pynchon wanted to draw a parallel to his treatment of V.: it is there and everybody "knows" that, but nobody can really claim to have seen it. Even Fausto, who alone saw V.—if he did—has to admit that she was in a state of decay and thus confirms the idea that V. (and, by extension, entropy) can be recognized only by its deadly effects. If this was indeed Pynchon's design, it was fundamentally altered in his next book, *The Crying of Lot 49*.

Entropy exists in this novel on several levels. The most obvious is the straightforward use of the term by several characters, frequently accompanied by discussions of other scientific notions. This verbal presence is rather self-explanatory and has been convincingly dealt with by many critics.[8] Yet some other aspects of the significance of entropy for *The Crying of Lot 49* are not so immediately evident, and are worth discussing at more length.

One area of "concealed" entropy is related to the notion of probability. We know that the more entropic a system, the greater the probability of its elements and the less information gained by learning about them. On the surface, the world of *The Crying of Lot 49* seems highly improbable, as the events described there defy our experience. We should not, however, mistake the uncommon for the improbable. Oedipa Maas' adventures are certainly most peculiar, but are they also totally unpredictable? The answer may be contained in Pynchon's unusual narrative mode.

The narration of *The Crying of Lot 49* seems to be limited to what Oedipa could know herself. The book's multiple puzzles remain unsolved because the readers are never allowed to look at the events from any point of view other than Oedipa's own. Yet if we examine the opening sentences of some of the chapters, we shall find that the first sentence of chapter 2 is: "She left Kinneret, then, with no idea she was moving toward anything new";[9] of chapter 3: "Things then did not delay in turning curious" (p. 44); of chapter 5: "Though her next move should have been to contact Randolph Driblette . . . "(p. 100)—and we should remember that Driblette died a strange death soon after. These constructions seem to convey the idea that while Oedipa may not know what to expect, whatever happens to and around her is predestined, and therefore its probability is high. Although Oedipa feels lost in her quest, she is in fact lost only in a highly organized structure, and both a high probability of events and a high level of organization are among the primary features of entropy.

One of the most revealing scenes occurs when Metzger makes Oedipa bet on the ending of the movie they are watching and in which Metzger presumably starred as a child-actor, Baby Igor. Oedipa first rejects the idea, as the movie has already been made and nothing can alter its plot. Metzger, however, replies: "But you still don't know. You haven't seen it" (p. 34), and prevails upon her. The scene exemplifies the relation between objective probability and one's subjective perception of it. Oedipa agrees to make the bet on what for her is a future course of events in which various endings are equally possible; yet it is the past she is talking about, and there exists no alternative to the situation that has already been decided upon. Similarly, she may be curious about and surprised at the way events develop, but in fact their sequence has been established in advance and there can be no variation. Interestingly enough, she is astonished to find out that the movie ends in what seems to be the most probable conclusion, rather than in an improbable Hollywood-type ending. Once again high probability, an indispensable quality of entropy, triumphs.

Another group of events and remarks that points to the entropic kernel of the book is related to the problem of communication, which is one of the most frequently addressed notions in the novel. When Oedipa approaches San Narciso she perceives the California road system as some special kind of pattern with "an intent to communicate" (p. 24), though she is never able to find such communication. Later, after she has discovered the muted horn, she keeps looking for signs, and when she finds none in a ladies' room she "[feels] threatened by this absence of even the marginal try at communication latrines are known for" (p. 70). She then attends a meeting of shareholders in the Yoyodyne factory, who sing their favorite song, entitled "Glee." Contrary to what might have been expected, it enumerates the business successes of other corporations and the misery of Yoyodyne, but Oedipa somehow does not notice the discrepancy between the occasion and the song's message. At one point Oedipa is persuaded to attend a ball for the deaf-mutes at which each pair dances to its own "music," as there would be no use for the common communication usually supplied on such occasions by a band or an electronic device. There are also numerous communication-related phenomena of an extraordinary nature which involve Oedipa and her husband. Mucho Maas, a victim of LSD experiments, boasts that he can divide a musical tune into an infinite number of separate channels, yet is unable to receive such a message in its meaningful entirety and understand it. Not only can Oedipa and Mucho communicate in a kind of telepathic transmission, but at one point Mucho's broadcast reaches Oedipa over a distance far too great for such a phenomenon to occur. Interviewing her for his station, Mucho gives the name of Oedipa Maas as Edna Mosh because, as he says, "It'll come out the right way. I was allowing for the distortion on these rigs, and then when they put it on tape" (p. 139).

Throughout the novel messages seem to abound, but they do not convey much useful or meaningful information. Oedipa thinks she learns new things constantly, but they lead nowhere; they do not help her solve any of the puzzles that she encounters. The communication process in the San Narciso reality has been eroded by entropy. The Tristero system, which was supposed to assure proper communication, is about to die the entropic death, too. It presumably still exists but no longer transmits any meaningful information. People are required to write letters just to keep the volume of mail at a respectable level, but casual greetings are all that they convey. This is the real end of Tristero: it may have survived wars and revolutions, internal struggle and persecution, but entropic death cannot be resisted. It is an irreversible process, and because the system has lost its meaning, Oedipa's attempts at uncovering the secrets of Tristero cannot be successful. The words WASTE and DEATH, once acronyms for menacing messages ("We Await Secret Tristero Empire" and "Don't Ever Antagonize The Horn") now simply describe what happened to the system, which died and turned to waste because of its own entropy. The only person Oedipa encounters who openly wears the Tristero's symbol reacts to her dramatic plea for an explanation by saying, "It's too late." "For me?" asks Oedipa, and gets an answer whose meaning escapes her: the man says, "For me," and hangs up on her (p. 177).

Entropy in *The Crying of Lot 49* can thus be seen both as its main organizing principle and as Pynchon's basic philosophical assumption. What remains is a possible discrepancy between what entropy of information is all about and the existence of the book itself. Even if the world described there is entropic, it would seem that by the very act of writing and reading about it, a certain amount of information is passed on, which would cause a decrease of entropy, at least locally. But— and this seems to be Pynchon's ultimate coup—*The Crying of Lot 49* conveys practically no such information. We do not learn anything about the characters that is not ambiguous. Not only are the Paranoids, Metzger, and Dr. Hilarious changing personalities in a way that does not permit any characterization, but we even know nothing about Oedipa herself except for some scattered, meaningless, and sometimes conflicting pieces of information. All events are treated in a similar way, and so is the location of the novel: while some geographical names are real (Los Angeles, Berkeley), the essential ones (San Narciso and Kinneret) are fictitious,[10] thus leaving open the question of the book's relation to reality. Apparently, Pynchon also plays a game with people's names. At first they seem to convey a message. Apart from Oedipa and Mucho, three employees of Yoyodyne are named Koteks, Fallopian, and Bloody Chiclitz; others bear names like Driblette, Di Presso, Genghis Cohen, Pierce Inverarity. However, a closer analysis reveals that there is no consistent pattern here, that we deal with a mixture of potentially meaningful names, Pynchon's own in-jokes, and names that are simply unusual or amusing but seem to convey no hidden meaning related to the novel's message.[11] Such messages, meant to confuse rather than communicate, can also be characterized as devoid of information, which would make them fully entropic. Another example here would be that of Mucho Maas, who is haunted and scared by a metal sign that reads "N.A.D.A." It is an acronym for National Automobile Dealers' Association but Mucho pronounces it as a word, "nada" (p. 144). Can this be interpreted as a Russian word for "one ought to," which would fit the situation very well? And is there any connection here with the fact that Oedipa's other man's alter ego is Baby Igor? Or perhaps it should be interpreted as a Spanish word for "nothing," which would then be consistent with Mucho's Spanish-sounding first name. The real question, however, is whether answers to such questions would add anything significant to our understanding of the book—and it seems that no matter which interpretation we choose, we shall not learn anything new about this novel. All such hints seem either to move in circles, or else lead nowhere, their only function being to provide empty clues which pass for information, otherwise absent from *The Crying of Lot 49*.

It is therefore possible to conclude that Pynchon has achieved the full entropic effect. He has not only incorporated entropy into the plot of his novel and made his characters constantly encounter its symptoms, but he has also reached the reader. As the amount of information decreases, entropy increases, and *The Crying of Lot 49* offers practically no information. The clues are misleading for Oedipa; they are empty for us as well. We read Pynchon's message, but having done so we seem to be left with little more than the knowledge of its existence. Norbert Wiener calls messages "a form of pattern and organization" which are measured by how much information a given set of messages carries.[12] Human beings, moreover, need information to fight their own entropy. Because Pynchon's *The Crying of Lot 49* offers no meaningful information, the book is not only a fictional scenario for entropic death, but also an instrument of increasing entropy among its readers. It is therefore not only a novel about entropy, but in fact an entropic novel, with its universe going through the process of disintegration and its readers being subjected to a significantly decreased supply of information.

With entropy established as the controlling metaphor in *V.* and *The Crying of Lot 49*, as well as in Pynchon's earlier stories, the appearance in 1973 of his third novel, *Gravity's Rainbow*, made his readers call upon the notion of entropy in their attempts to penetrate the book's puzzling message. One obviously mistaken opinion notwithstanding,[13] entropy's presence in the book was also generally recognized by the critics. At the same time, however, it became evident that *Gravity's Rainbow* is a book far too complex to have its meaning explained by the application of only one concept. While entropy remains one of Pynchon's main ideas, it appears in this book as part of a larger concept, science, which is present both as a metaphor and as a subject *per se*, and is discussed in the novel's numerous encyclopaedic digressions. The novel can therefore be best explained not by one concept, but by a set of science-related notions, such as entropy, relativity, gravity, the Rocket, and technological control.

The term *entropy*, so eminent in *The Crying of Lot 49*, appears in *Gravity's Rainbow* only a few times, usually in neutral contexts that refer to its common-sense meaning rather than to its scientific one, such as "He wants to preserve what he can of her from Their several entropies, from Their softsoaping and Their money."[14] Also, some other entropy-related terms are occasionally used in meaningful contexts: "Destruction, oh, and demons—yes, including Maxwell's—were there, deep in the woods, with other beasts vaulting among the earthworks of your safety" (p. 239). It may also be pointed out that with entropy being symbolized in physics by the letter S, S-shaped structures and figures appear with considerable frequency in the book. But despite the

scarcity of direct references, entropy is *Gravity's Rainbow*'s main philosophical and structural principle—in the same way that the principle
of mimesis has been in so many novels. Even more than Pynchon's
earlier books, *Gravity's Rainbow* lacks a traditional, progressing plot,
has hundreds of characters but no main hero (or so many main heroes
that the term is rendered meaningless), moves freely in time and space
regardless of the ensuing confusion—all this in a deliberate effort not
so much to portray our reality, as mimetic literature would, as to present
a hypothesized world under the reign of entropy.

The first chapter of *Gravity's Rainbow* is titled "Beyond the Zero"
and at its very beginning we come across the following statement:

a sour smell of rolling-stock absence, of maturing rust, developing through
those emptying days brilliant and deep, especially at dawn, with blue shadows
to seal its passage, to try to bring events to Absolute Zero. (p. 3)

Entropy does not necessarily lead to Absolute Zero, yet the random
distribution of energy will also render all work impossible, as there will
be no "events" any more: "One possible connotation of . . . Final Zero
is absolute zero, a condition that arrests entropy's increase but hardly
offers any viable alternative—even as an unattainable ideal condition."[15] "Beyond the Zero" as the title of the opening chapter could
thus suggest that the narrative takes place after entropy's final victory.
Such a time framework, which would contradict the principle of ultimate
inertness resulting from the heat death, seems to have been introduced
with a specific purpose: to underscore the novel's specific, inverted
treatment of both the chronology and the cause-and-effect chain.

One of the main lines of events in *Gravity's Rainbow* is triggered by
the fact that a certain Tyrone Slothrop, an American who works for
one of the wartime intelligence agencies in England, has a habit of
marking the map of London with stars signifying his love conquests.
As it happens, the map of V-2 hits corresponds exactly to Slothrop's
map. What makes the concurrence impossible to explain in rational
terms is that Slothrop's affairs do not follow the rocket strikes, but
precede them by a few days. What could be easily explained as an
effect becomes a mysterious cause. Neither is this the only "reversed"
relation in the book. Tchitcherine's belief in the existence of the Coun-
terforce (caused, as it was, by Slothrop's being dressed in a Red Army
uniform) brings it to life; van Goll's seemingly surrealistic film about

Schwartzkommando is followed by a revelation that there is indeed an
African unit in the Aryan German army; the conditioning of Dog Vanya
has reached the ''equivalent'' stage in which ''a stronger stimulus no
longer gets a stronger response'' (p. 79); one of the most frequently
discussed features of the V-2 rockets is that they are faster than sound
so that the strikes precede the screaming. The basic reason for all these
''reversed'' phenomena is that entropy and the cause-and-effect relation
cannot co-exist. Consequently, if the former prevails, the latter has to
be abandoned:

There's a feeling about that cause-and-effect may have been taken as far as it
will go. That for science to carry on at all, it must look for a less narrow, a
less ... sterile set of assumptions. The next great breakthrough may come
when we have the courage to junk cause-and-effect entirely. (p. 89)

Occasionally, Pynchon acknowledges more traditional expectations
(''You will want cause and effect. All right.'' [p. 663]) and introduces
what can be described as plots into *Gravity's Rainbow*, but the overall
picture is that of the dissipation of events. The main figure of one such
plot, Slothrop, is not only cut off from the events of his world, but
eventually dissolves in time. Scott Sanders observes that ''the only
prospect more terrifying than being caught in Gravity's entropic tide,
than being the object of a cosmic plot, is standing outside all plots,
swimming free of all tides.''[16] While the assessment is very much to
the point, it must also be stressed that ''swimming free of all tides'' is
in itself entropic, that the ultimate state of both organization and disorder
signified by entropy also precludes all meaningful relationships, makes
one either disappear physically (Slothrop again, but also Enzian, and,
in a sense, Tchitcherine), or feel totally lost in the environment—which
in turn is neither hostile nor friendly, but simply alien to one's needs.
 Once the cause-and-effect relation has disappeared everything becomes relative, reduced to being a function of the character's projection
of his wishes upon the unreliable environment. Successive stages of
V.'s plot are carefully dated, and the sequence of events in *The Crying
of Lot 49* is easier to establish than almost anything else in the book.
In *Gravity's Rainbow* only the most general frame of chronological
reference is known, and even here a certain duality appears. While we
would be inclined to characterize this frame as the end of World War

II, it should in fact be recognized as something else: the Rocket time. One of the images used to visualize Einstein's concept of the relativity of time is that of two twins, one of whom is placed in a rocket travelling close to the speed of light and who therefore ages more slowly. In *Gravity's Rainbow* Gottfried is launched in the 00000 Rocket, while Enzian may yet take his place in the 00001 rockets, and disproportionate importance is attached to the fact that both are said to have siblings: Katje and Tchitcherine, respectively. Actually, these pairs are not related, but the question is given plenty of attention and the problem of having a sibling becomes one of the most frequently discussed in the novel.

The idea of the Rocket time also has another meaning. Almost all of the book's events, however loosely connected, are nonetheless related in time—and frequently in essence—to the Rocket. Slothrop wants to find the S-Gerat and Imipolex G. Enzian wants to assemble rocket 00001. Pirate Prentice tries to gather intelligence data about V-2. Tchitcherine is after Slothrop, Enzian, and all that they are after. Katje helps to destroy launching pads. All of them live by the Rocket and when the last rocket is put together and launched, thus concluding the Rocket time, they all die, disappear, or otherwise pass into oblivion.

Ironically, this relativistic framework is subordinated to the most Newtonian of forces: gravity. In a way gravity is even more sinister than entropy. While the latter can be locally stopped or even temporarily reversed, the former binds everybody and everything at all times. "Within the structure of Pynchon's social speculations, gravity in the macrocosm corresponds to the mechanism of repression in the little world of man, the microcosm," observes Lawrence C. Wolfley.[17] While he may be exaggerating the role of gravity in *Gravity's Rainbow*, there is little doubt that its power extends over more than the world of physics: "Gravity becomes the paranoid God, wreaking destruction upon an entire cosmos imagined, in Puritan terms, as innately depraved."[18]

The world of *Gravity's Rainbow* is depraved not only in the Puritan sense, and its destruction seems to be justly deserved. Yet Pynchon does not pass any moral judgements in the book; he substitutes for them the inevitable reign of physical forces. Sinners were at the mercy of an angry God who felt only contempt for them, but while Edwards' audience was frightened, it could understand the danger. Gravity is a depersonalized and merciless power; to construct the book's central metaphor around it is to deprive both the characters and the readers of all hope. Gottfried is the most passive figure in *Gravity's Rainbow*, while Enzian is one of the most active, yet gravity treats them alike, and neither can survive a crash against the undifferentiating surface.

Unlike entropy, however, gravity is not exclusively a destructive force. By pulling all bodies into its reign, it provides a common basis that holds us together when other links fail. Slothrop sees plots everywhere, but they do not frighten him. What he is really afraid of is to be left out of all connections, entirely to himself, with no *Them* to hold responsible for whatever happens to him. Slothrop also wants to have his existence confirmed, as he tries to get the papers, and hopes to regain his long-lost identity. But all these attempts fail. He begins "to thin, to scatter," and even gravity begins to lose its control over him. Finally there is no plot around him to justify his existence. Anti-paranoia establishes itself as a destructive power, and Slothrop disintegrates, gravity having nothing to hold together anymore.

Gravity's Rainbow is frequently described as a book of opposites, a series of permanent struggles between contradictory tendencies and forces. Chaos and order fight a hopeless battle which can end only in entropic death. Paranoia and anti-paranoia compete for the inescapable destruction of man. Everybody seems to be engaged in an antagonistic relationship with somebody else. Gravity is no exception, and its main adversary is the Rocket.

While rockets are destructive, the idea of the Rocket as presented in the book is in fact the embodiment of forces, of possibilities, and of hope that people may still have in their unequal struggle against physical forces and man-made dangers. Perhaps the best exposition of the Rocket's role comes when Enzian, a future Rocket operator and its ultimate victim, is brought to Europe by Weissmann-Blicero, a man more closely related to the Rocket than anybody else in the book:

Beyond simple steel erection, the Rocket was an entire system *won*, away from the feminine darkness, held against the entropies of lovable but scatterbrained Mother Nature: that was the first thing he was obliged by Weissmann to learn, his first step toward citizenship in the Zone. He was led to believe that by understanding the Rocket, he would come to understand truly his manhood. (p. 324)

And toward the end of the book:

But the Rocket has to be many things, it must answer to a number of different shapes in the dreams of those who touch it—in combat, in tunnel, on paper— it must survive heresies shining, unconfoundable . . . and heretics there will be. (p. 727)

The Rocket embodies what constitutes life itself: love, hatred, death; and it is present at all the important events of the book. Like the forces of gravity, which never cease to work, their adversary, the Rocket, is conspicuous in the world of *Gravity's Rainbow* from the opening ''A screaming comes across the sky'' to the final descent upon the cinema house in which we all sit. The 00001 rocket is the last one there is; Enzian is the last person who not only can operate it, but who also understands it and believes in it; and after

the pointed tip of the Rocket, falling nearly a mile per second, absolutely and forever without sound, reaches its last unmeasurable gap above the roof of this old theatre . . . (p. 760)

the world will be deprived of the only force capable of challenging gravity, and will thus be destroyed. Gravity will triumph once again, but the unanswered question is whether this victory can avoid becoming self-destructive. In a world based on opposites, where permanent struggle is the only *raison d'être*, to be deprived of one's foe may be tantamount to death. Margherita Erdmann begs to be beaten so that she can be reassured she is still alive; Roger Mexico survives as long as he has Pointsman as his professional opponent and Jeremy as his personal one; Slothrop dissolves when nobody is after him any longer—can gravity destroy the Rocket and survive? V. was dismantled, but her searchers survived; we leave *The Crying of Lot 49* before the secret is revealed; but the end of *Gravity's Rainbow* also signifies the end of the world.

Just as *The Crying of Lot 49* is more than a book about entropy: it is an entropic book, *Gravity's Rainbow* is more than a book that utilizes science: it wants to embody it. To be more precise, just as the entropic process in *The Crying of Lot 49* transcended the limits of the fictional world of the book, *Gravity's Rainbow* is preoccupied with science to the point of going beyond the human beings that created it and reaching to inanimate matter and primordial forces. The book is full of serious and accurate references to science, but almost all scientists presented there are fools, perverts, maniacs. Pynchon respects the physical world, but not the people. The Rocket is man-made and is meant to conquer the most powerful force of nature, gravity. But gravity stands up to the challenge, wins, and leaves us all dead.

In the complex scientific vision of *Gravity's Rainbow*, entropy is no longer the only ominous force. This does not mean, however, that entropy is any less imminent, that the world can escape it. The Rocket was constructed as a symbol of hope "held against the entropies of Nature"—and it failed. Gravity is capable of quick and dramatic physical destruction, but entropy will continue to dissolve things and bring about their decay, so that even the ruins of civilization, which gravity's forces have left to bear witness to its power, will disappear.

NOTES

1. See in particular Joseph W. Slade, *Thomas Pynchon*; see also a revised chapter included as " 'Entropy' and Other Calamities" in Edward Mendelson, ed., *Pynchon*, pp. 69-86.

2. Thomas Pynchon, "Entropy," p. 292.

3. Tony Tanner, "Caries and Cabals," in *City of Words*, pp. 153-80.

4. Thomas Pynchon, *V.*, p. 268. Subsequent references in parentheses are to this edition.

5. Richard Patteson, "What Stencil Knew: Structure and Certitude in Pynchon's *V.*" p. 39.

6. Edward Mendelson, "The Sacred, the Profane and *The Crying of Lot 49*," in Kenneth H. Baldwin and David K. Kirby, eds., *Individual and Community*, p. 200.

7. W. T. Lhamon, Jr., "Pentecost, Promiscuity, and Pynchon's *V.*: From the Scaffold to the Impulsive," in George Levine and David Leverenz, eds., *Mindful Pleasures*, pp. 73-74.

8. Cf. Peter Abernathy, "Entropy in Pynchon's *The Crying of Lot 49*," pp. 18-33; Thomas R. Lyons and Allan D. Franklin, "Thomas Pynchon's 'Classic' Presentation of the Second Law of Thermodynamics," pp. 195-204; Anne Mangel, "Maxwell's Demon, Entropy, Information: *The Crying of Lot 49*," pp. 194-208; William M. Plater, *The Grim Phoenix*; Neil Schmitz, "Describing the Demon: The Appeal of Thomas Pynchon," pp. 112-25; Joseph W. Slade, *Thomas Pynchon*; James Dean Young, "The Enigma Variations of Thomas Pynchon," pp. 69-77.

9. Thomas Pynchon, *The Crying of Lot 49*, p. 23. Subsequent references in parentheses are to this edition.

10. It is interesting to note in this context that Tanner refers to San Narciso

as San Narcisco throughout his *City of Words*; John P. Leland makes the same mistake in his article, "Pynchon's Linguistic Demon: *The Crying of Lot 49*," p. 45.

11. For interesting remarks on Pynchon's onomastic practices, see Leland, "Pynchon's Linguistic Demon," pp. 48-49, and Young, "Enigma Variations," pp. 71-72.

12. Norbert Wiener, *The Human Use of Human Beings*, p. 21.

13. Scott Simmon, "*Gravity's Rainbow* Described," pp. 54-67.

14. Thomas Pynchon, *Gravity's Rainbow*, p. 302. Subsequent references in parentheses are to this edition.

15. Plater, *Grim Phoenix*, p. 247.

16. Scott Sanders, "Pynchon's Paranoid History," in *Mindful Pleasures*, p. 151.

17. Lawrence C. Wolfley, "Repression Rainbow: The Presence of Norman O. Brown in Pynchon's Big Novel," p. 876.

18. Sanders, "Paranoid History," pp. 150-51.

8

THREE DIMENSIONS OF ENTROPY: WILLIAM GADDIS, SUSAN SONTAG, JOHN UPDIKE

Thomas Pynchon devotes less attention to informational entropy than to physical entropy: disintegration of language seems to be a less terrifying vision than the decay of the world. However, a breakdown of communication among people could also result in the collapse of our civilization, so in order to get a fuller picture of the entropic threat, it may be worthwhile to discuss a novel where informational entropy is given more consideration.

William Gaddis' *JR*, published in 1975, marks a significant change in his preoccupations as a writer. His only previous work, *The Recognitions*, published in 1955 and widely considered to be one of the very few truly important postwar American novels, was devoted to the basic relation between the true and the false, the original and the fake; to the manner in which we comprehend, recreate, and transform the world. The topic of Gaddis' second novel is entropy, or chaos versus order. The plot of the book is quite simple: a thirteen-year-old boy, called JR (for "junior") by his classmates, combines shrewdness with true naïveté and, operating mainly from the school's pay telephone, establishes—by design as well as by coincidence—a huge nationwide business conglomerate. His "family of companies" in fact resembles Inverarity's emporium in *The Crying of Lot 49*, and the ludicrous ineptness of the people who help JR run it (he has not even quit school in the process) is not unlike Oedipa Maas' or Metzger's awkward attempts at carrying out Inverarity's last will. *JR* is a brilliant satire on the American industrial and financial complex, a bitter comment on the educational system, an American book of manners—but first of all it is a novel about entropy taking hold of the world.

The notion of entropy is introduced directly in one of the book's opening scenes, in which a physics lesson is transmitted to classrooms over a closed-circuit television system. A teacher named Gibbs suddenly interrupts a discussion of the First Law of Thermodynamics and asks the children about the Second Law, which they have not studied yet. It may not be a coincidence that Gibbs was also the name of the American physicist who prepared the way for the discovery of entropy and who figures very prominently in Wiener's *The Human Use of Human Beings*. The teacher proceeds to introduce ("discover") the notion and says:

You ... assume that organization is an inherent property of the knowledge itself, and that disorder and chaos are simply irrelevant forces that threaten it from outside. In fact it's exactly the opposite. Order is simply a thin, perilous condition we try to impose on the basic reality of chaos.[1]

The children do not understand anything of what he says. Frustrated, Gibbs adds:

You're not here to learn anything, but to be taught so you can pass these tests, knowledge has to be organized so it can be taught and it has to be reduced to information so it can be organized. (p. 20)

In other words, the world is inherently chaotic and knowledge is reduced to information. These two assumptions subsequently become the basic principles of *JR*'s world.

To understand the reality of the book, we should remember Planck's statement that "elementary disorder [is] ... the preliminary condition for the existence of entropy."[2] JR enters the world of business and finance, which is supposed to be highly organized, but his first encounter with it clearly contradicts this belief. When his class goes for a field trip to corporate headquarters, it appears that chaos, rather than order, is the ruling principle there. Children are given classified memos, film projectors run backwards or not at all, the boardroom leaks, important documents are misplaced. When the JR Family of Companies grows into a $500 million operation, it has understandably "perfected" the chaos. Its own office is located in a one-bedroom apartment where a picture telephone and modern office machines have been installed. But the door does not open; water cannot be turned off; shares are kept in a refrigerator; the whole room is filled with different cartons which in turn cover a radio that cannot be reached and switched off; pounds of business letters are delivered daily and never opened; somebody tries to unload 100,000 plastic flowers; two young people make love; and another character tries to compose a symphony. This is how entropy proceeds: elementary disorder, once introduced, will make all things deteriorate until finally the whole world disintegrates.

The motif of disintegration and decay, of everything turning into waste or junk, recurs throughout the book. One of the main items on a high school budget is repairs; people say that ''America's all about waste disposal'' (p. 27); and on a school television system Smokey Bear encourages a ''pledge as an American to save and faithfully to defend from waste'' (p. 38). Gibbs refers to his own carefully prepared notes as ''junk'' (p. 487), and when somebody dictates a text over the telephone it comes out as '' . . . in conjunction with . . . no, conjunction, conjunk, junk . . .'' (p. 28); some people still try to argue that ''waste shows an undisciplined strain of mind'' (p. 110), but obviously it is too late. Junk, refuse, and waste will pile up, energy will not stop leaking until—in Gibbs' words—differences are ''homogenized,'' everything becomes perfectly alike, and entropy triumphs.

The disintegration of the material world must influence people who live in it. While some seem able to move around in this chaos, or even understand it, their behavior only increases entropy. The entropic process is considerably accelerated by the activities of characters like JR, Governor Cates, and Montcrieff, all of whom seem to enjoy the confusion they create, or Mr. Davidoff, who pretends he is in control of events, whereas he only compounds the general disorder. Others, like Mrs. Joubert or Edward Bast, try to stop the process but their efforts are invariably futile; and some people have already become victims of entropy. One such man is Mr. Duncan, who says he had fought a hopeless battle for years, but was finally forced out of business by the JR Corporation (the primary vehicle of entropy). He disintegrates in a hospital, having been left with no money and no hope, only a fraudulent insurance policy issued by one of JR's subsidiaries. In fact, his death resembles another classic scene of entropic decay—the death of the Soldier in White in Joseph Heller's *Catch-22*. The main difference, however, is that while the Soldier in White was turned into a closed system and disintegrated "inward," Duncan seems to dissolve into words. For the last few days of his life he does not stop talking, regardless of whether anybody listens to him or not. He becomes all words, in a way that strongly suggests that informational entropy is the real cause of his death—and the main theme of the book.

JR's particular concern is the communication process, and almost all of its 725 pages consist of dialogue. But while everybody wants to convey messages to everybody else, almost no one succeeds. Knowledge is being reduced to information to facilitate the communication process, but while plenty of messages are being sent—by various char-. acters, by TV and radio, whose programs frequently accompany conversations, by means of print—people have trouble receiving them because of the overwhelming informational noise. However, the chaos that results has almost no negative impact upon people's behavior, because everybody seems to act upon signals rather than meaningful information. Anybody who can use the code is in a position to give orders even if he does not really know what the signals mean: JR's key to success is that he is uncommonly clever at using business gibberish. He does not really understand it, but others react with habitual obedience and never question his authority.

It is only natural that in such circumstances communication tools acquire a special significance, and the telephone plays a particularly important role in *JR*. It is in a sense the main hero of the book and its omnipresence directly influences events. JR, for example, can talk to his business associates and rivals only on the telephone, because by stuffing a handkerchief into the receiver or playing prerecorded statements at a lower speed he can change his voice and thus conceal his age. The telephone, instead of being only a tool, thus performs an active role by hiding the true identity of the people who use it. Consequently, the message is falsified in the process of transmission and the information received cannot be considered reliable. Everybody in the book talks on the telephone with somebody else, and frequently with more than one party at a time, but these conversations do not serve the purpose of exchanging information. The telephone is in itself a message, and its ringing an order to behave in an accustomed way, while the fact that people place the receiver on a table and let the other party keep talking does not seem to stop the constant flow of words, which become empty, useless messages. In the book's final scene JR is talking on the telephone but there is nobody at the other end. He finally realizes it, and the book closes with: "So I mean listen I got this neat idea hey, you listening? Hey? You listening . . . ?" Nobody listens, but the JR operation will certainly proceed regardless, and it is only a matter of time before people fully submit to the power of the telephone: there is some talk already about it being able to transmit human beings. *JR* opens with the word "money," which in the beginning seems to be its main concern, but when it ends we realize that the telephone has in fact become not only the book's main metaphor, but possibly the governing power of its universe as well.

The novel's two central images, that of junk, and that of the informational waste created by the surplus of messages, converge in the "scientific" idea concocted by Mr. Davidoff, himself the book's greatest contributor to the increase of junk and noise. In a characteristically convoluted manner he comes up with the following "press release":

The still secret Frigicom process is attracting the attention of our major cities as the latest scientific breakthrough promising noise elimination by the placement of absorbing screens at what are called quote shard intervals unquote in noise polluted areas period operating at faster hyphen than hyphen sound speeds comma a complex process employing liquid nitrogen will be used to convert the noise shards comma as they are known comma at temperatures so low they may be handled with comparative ease by trained personnel immediately upon emission before the noise element is released into the atmosphere period the shards will then be collected and disposed of in remote areas or at sea comma where the disturbance caused by their thawing will make that where no one will be disturbed by their impact upon thawing period new paragraph. (p. 527)

The scientific "merits" of this procedure aside, it again represents a typical entropy-creating reasoning. Instead of liquidating the sources of noise, an increase of waste is being suggested, which could only bring about an increase of entropy. Richard Brautigan's wrecking yards, Thomas Pynchon's WASTE, and William Gaddis' noise disposal are all parts of the same concept, according to which our world is being turned into a gigantic junk heap where nothing new can be born and which can only await decomposition and entropic death.

Jack Gibbs says at one point in the book: "Read Wiener on communication, more complicated the message more God damned chance for errors" (p. 403). Yet the picture that emerges from *JR* is not that of errors caused by the increased flow of information, but of the irreversible process of entropic decay and disintegration of people, objects, and information. *JR* is certainly an entertaining book, full of humorous scenes and comical characters, but its overall message is unquestionably pessimistic. Errors, mistakes, inaccuracies can all be corrected, but a logical consequence of a physical process cannot be avoided. Particularly so, Gaddis says at the end of his book, since nobody is listening.

Susan Sontag's *Death Kit*, on the other hand, does not concern itself with the presence or absence of a listener. It describes the journey of Diddy, the main character, into himself, which is paralleled by his "real" excursions into tunnels and other enclosed areas. The narrative is basically in the third person singular, but occasionally switches into the first person plural, so that we cannot be certain about the identity of the narrator. Moreover, there is enough evidence in the book to presume that all "events" occur only in Diddy's dying mind after he has swallowed half a bottle of sleeping pills. Consequently, the sphere of "reality" is not clearly delineated, and even distinctly marked dream scenes can in fact be dreams-within-dreams.

Death Kit is built around the metaphor of running down—both of Diddy's life and of the world around him. His days used to be almost pedantically organized, and he himself is "a mild fellow, gently reared in a middle-sized city in Pennsylvania and expensively educated."[3] Gradually, however, things that surround Diddy begin to run down, and the tension increases to the point where he tries to commit suicide. He recovers (or rather "apparently" does) and takes a business trip, and while his train is stalled in a tunnel, he murders a railroad worker (or so he believes, as it may have been only a dream). On the same train he meets a blind girl, Hester, becomes attached to her, and makes her move in with him. In order to free himself from the murder image, he takes Hester back to the tunnel, re-enacts the murder, and, after a violent love-making scene, enters another tunnel which is in fact a mysterious succession of corridors full of dead people and objects.[4]

Diddy's withdrawal and decay are paralleled by the general "running down" of the outside world:

Everything is bound to run down. The walls sag. Empty spaces bulge between objects. The surfaces of objects sweat, thin out, buckle. The hysterical fluids of fear deposited at the core of objects ooze out along the seams. ... (p. 2)

Diddy seems less and less able to cope with the decay of once familiar structures. The only defense he can find is to shut himself in, but while this gives him temporary protection, he risks turning into a closed system and succumbing to entropy. When Diddy takes a train trip, he travels in "European compartments" that take only a few passengers rather than in open carriages. Once he reaches his destination, he spends most of his time in a hotel room and declines all invitations. When he and Hester get back to New York, he first tries to give her a sense of the neighborhood, but soon they both withdraw to his apartment, which they try not to leave. He even gives away his beloved dog, so that he will not have to walk it, and refuses to let his brother in when the latter calls on him; while Hester is really blind, Diddy moves around his apartment with his eyes closed so that he can intensify the feeling of isolation and minimize the amount of information received through sense organs. When he almost refuses to eat, too, we are again reminded of Wiener's thesis that human beings are not closed systems because they take in food and sensory data: Diddy has decided to give up both and becomes vulnerable to entropy.

The book ends with Diddy's death, and it is obvious that he finally surrenders to the forces he cannot control, that "deliquescent running-down of everything [becomes] co-existent with Diddy's entire span of consciousness" (p. 3). JR was totally oblivious to the inner world, to concepts like beauty or harmony; his world was the world of action and messages. Diddy, on the other hand, seems to disregard the world around him as long as nothing interferes with the privacy of his mind. However, once this sphere is violated, Diddy is unable to defend himself and gives in almost without resistance. Entropy can cause the decay of the whole informational process and thus destroy human beings by preventing them from communicating with others; it can also achieve a similarly destructive result by dissolving one's mind. At the end of the book Diddy's body dies, but this seems an almost insignificant consequence of the earlier disintegration of his mental processes. While "intellectual" entropy seems to be able to threaten only certain types of people, it can in fact affect all human beings who, like Diddy, reject the outside world by refusing to take in new information. It is, therefore, no less dangerous than informational entropy, even though its destructive power seems to originate within afflicted individuals rather than outside them.

The effect of the threat that Gaddis and Sontag (as well as Pynchon) try to convey is somewhat diminished by the exceptionalness of their worlds: the characters of Pynchon's novels live in worlds almost unrelated to our everyday experience, and those of Gaddis' *JR* and Sontag's *Death Kit* are put in extreme situations. The reality portrayed in these books, while recognizable, does not quite resemble the reality of our immediate experience, making it difficult for the reader to identify with the people and processes described there. This, in turn, leads to the question of whether the entropic process can really take place in the "normal" world we all know, and, if it can, what shape it is likely to assume. At least a partial answer seems to be provided by John Updike's novels.

Updike's characters live in the realistic environment of Middle America, and as a result the reader is faced not with a more or less imaginary danger, but with a very real one. Instead of destroying a mysterious Tristero system, the destructive process has taken control over the normal eight-to-five, Monday-through-Friday suburban America. Moreover, in contrast to, for instance, Saul Bellow's Herzog, whose passiveness can only partially be ascribed to entropy, or Norman Mailer's heroes, who seem to be preoccupied with only one of its aspects—the opposition between Manichean and Augustinian evil—Updike places entropy in the very center of his novels. It controls his world and stops just short of bringing about its total destruction, with some characters having already succumbed to its power. One such figure is Harry Angstrom, the hero of both *Rabbit, Run* (1960) and *Rabbit Redux* (1971), who struggles in vain against a force that he himself can neither name nor understand, but which possesses all the characteristic features of entropy.

In the earlier novel, Harry keeps running. He runs away from his wife three times and from his lover twice, but while running away seems simple, he cannot find anything to run toward. He leaves his wife, Janice, to run into Ruth, who becomes his lover—only to leave Ruth and return to Janice. Harry is always on the move; he never stops, as if he were afraid of even a momentary pause. Immobility facilitates entropy and thus helps destroy human beings, but what Harry does not realize is that repeated, aimless movement is equally useless as a counter-entropic strategy. In order to resist the process, one has to devise a meaningful activity and organize one's life around it, "transform motion into direction"—as Tony Tanner puts it—but Harry cannot do it. When he runs away for the first time, he really tries to leave everything behind and start anew. What happens, however, is that—like so many American characters before him—he falls victim to an overwhelming organization: in his case it is this perfect model of the all-embracing yet empty structure, the highway system. He keeps driving but instead of getting away from his home in Brewer, he only circles around it. "The only way to get somewhere, you know, is to figure out where you're going before you go there,"[5] says an old farmer of whom Harry asks directions, but the advice goes unheeded. Rabbit is unable to decide what he runs toward, so wherever he turns he can only find structures which are just like the ones he has left behind. It takes him several such trips to understand the hopelessness of his efforts and the inevitability of his fate:

There are so many red lines and blue lines, long names, little towns, squares and circles and stars.... The names melt away and he sees the map whole, a net, all those red lines and blue lines and stars, a net he is somewhere caught in. (pp. 35-36)

This is how Rabbit perceives America, which "from shore to shore was the same." He does not feel attracted by it, yet at the same time he cannot stay in Brewer, because it has lost the human dimension and has become all brick and waste, senseless multiplication and trash:

He comes into Brewer from the south, seeing it as a gradual multiplication of houses among the trees beside the road and then as a treeless waste of industry, shoe factories and bottling plants and company parking lots and knitting mills converted to electronics parts and elephantine gas tanks lifting above trash-filled swampland. (p. 39)

The imagery is familiar and, like so many times before, the wasted world signifies death. Janice Angstrom drowns her own daughter; Harry works in Mrs. Smith's garden but when he quits the job she tells him she will die before the flowers bloom again; he suddenly realizes that his old baseball coach, Tothero, and Ruth "both remind him of death." Rabbit himself comes close to disintegration: he almost stops eating, rejects everybody, can find no goal worth pursuing. He neither wants to nor is able to "come to grips" which, according to Tothero, is the whole secret of survival. He slowly dissolves and—as in other entropic novels—his state is contagious. During their last night together, Rabbit forces Ruth to perform a demeaning and destructive sex act during which she realizes that "this last month she's felt cold all the time" (p. 187). Harry makes the impression of living off people, and death seems to provide him with new energy. Even this, however, does not constitute a permanent solution: at the end of the book he attends his daughter's funeral, but when he runs away from the cemetery he can find no place to hide from entropy and death. Yet what makes Harry different from characters like Diddy is that even after he is defeated he still refuses to abandon hope. When Harry reappears ten years later in *Rabbit Redux*, he has learned that running does not help, but still believes that entropy can be stopped, or at least delayed, by acquiescence.

While his running away was at least some kind of revolt, Harry's behavior is now based on the principle of total and willing submission. He does not try to fight back but quietly accepts a succession of blows coming from all sides. His wife leaves him; he is talked into an affair with a hippie, Jill, and has to accept her militant black friend, who destroys them all; neighbors set his house on fire; he loses his job; his sister humiliates him—it seems that anywhere he turns he can expect only destruction and decay. Harry nonetheless holds on to his belief that there is some hidden order in the events and that if he can preserve it he will survive: "I need to keep things orderly or they get to me."[6] Faced with the dual threat of chaos and organization, the Rabbit of ten years before chose the former and got nowhere—and now he turns to the latter.

His problems can be best diagnosed as total entropy. He is still young and seemingly full of energy, but he cannot convert this energy into work. There are no extremes for him any longer, no polarizing experiences. He accepts his misfortunes and luck with equal indifference. He has even ceased to believe in the sexual energy that seemed to guide him in *Rabbit, Run*. At the end of *Rabbit Redux* he lies in bed with his wife, oblivious to what happens to him, reduced to a "human thing," and impotent. Harry's decay is more meaningful than Slothrop's or Diddy's because its physical aspect is enriched by a moral dimension. He was brought up in a strongly religious atmosphere, believing in the opposition between good and bad, virtue and sin, God and Devil. Yet in his own world such oppositions do not mean much any longer; they have dissolved into an indifferent acceptance of everything. Just as physical entropy renders all work impossible by levelling out the energy of the system, it is by cancelling differences between good and bad that moral entropy deprives human behavior of its meaning. Harry has an affair with his wife's best friend, his sister goes to bed with his wife's lover, and nobody minds. A vicious teenager destroys Harry's life and causes the death of his lover, and Harry helps him escape. An eighteen-year-old girl is burned to death, and all her family can think of is how to retrieve her white Porsche. Rabbit tries to understand everybody, and strives to free himself from prejudices—racial and otherwise—but in the process he deprives himself of standards. He tries to rely on organizing his life around the principle of love and acceptance, but ends up in chaos more overwhelming than that of ten years before.

Harry is a product of Middle America; his education and knowledge are limited; he also has, as Jill says, a "Puritan fear of waste"—all of which make him almost immune to the threats of intellectual or material entropy. What Updike seems to say, therefore, is that the danger can reach even deeper. In order to survive, a human being needs not only a habitable universe and meaningful information, but also moral standards. While other contemporary American novelists seem oblivious to this aspect of entropic threat, Updike considers it to be of primary importance and returns to it in at least one other novel, *Couples* (1968).

Unlike the Rabbit novels, *Couples* is not centered around one character but is an attempt to portray a typical East coast suburb, Tarbox. The novel's ostensible theme is sex, in various and frequently perverse configurations, yet it would be more accurate to say that *Couples* is a book about the disintegration, or entropy, of higher feelings, including moral standards. In one of the opening scenes the assembled couples try to remember the title of Edgar Allan Poe's story about a man whose cell walls kept squeezing in and they jocularly come up with " 'The Day the Walls Squeezed In' by I.M. Flat, a survivor in two dimensions."[7] A similar statement can be made about the Tarbox couples. They keep on working and making love, but as their third dimension, the moral sense, deteriorates and dissolves, "the boatyard crowd go[es] from decay to disintegration" (p. 109). They try to survive "in two dimensions," but they come to realize that this is not possible. Consequently, the couples become preoccupied with death; are "obsessed with decay"; believe that "to live is to lose"; realize that the existence machine can "run only one way. Downhill"; know that they "die all the time, in every direction." As a depressing but logical consequence, their children learn the facts of death even before they learn the facts of life. Nancy, Piet Hanema's little daughter, is constantly faced with death—of people, of favorite pets, of birds—which she first refuses to acknowledge, but soon grows to accept. Nancy is also the one who seems to understand the irreversibility of the entropic process. In a scene that is strongly reminiscent of Pynchon's "Entropy," Nancy brings home a frozen bird. Unlike Callisto, however, she evidently has no illusions about people being able to reverse the laws of physics when she says: "I'm going to put it on the radiator to get warm and come alive again even though I know it won't" (p. 351).

What makes the disintegration of the Tarbox world (and also of the world at large, since Updike frequently stresses the parallels between them) even more inescapable and permanent is that it is brought about by civilization. One of the book's final scenes is a powerful description of a church set on fire by lightning. There is some talk about rebuilding the church, but the final decision "is that the new building will not be a restoration but a modern edifice, a parabolic poured-concrete tent-shape peaked like a breaking wave" (pp. 456-457). The old values dissolve and are replaced by new ones.

The entropic process, unlike the apocalypse, leads to destruction rather than to the birth of new values, and in this respect *Couples* (as well as *Marry Me*, a somewhat similar novel of eight years later) does not carry the vision to its inescapable conclusion. Yet there can be no doubt that Updike's message is entropic, not only because he gives his characters names such as Maxwell and Gibbs, but primarily because his perspective is concentrated not on the material sphere, but on the moral one, where no rebirth occurs and where entropy is taking its prey. Updike's world is based on morals, and in Tarbox they have disintegrated. What is left is not another shell of the physical world, but ashes. Updike's man cannot survive in two dimensions. If he loses his moral standards he ceases to exist as a human being even if his "flat" body survives. The closed system of ten couples perishes because entropy's hold on morals can be just as persistent and deadly as it is on the physical world and on the informational process.

The term *entropy*, as used in literary studies, cannot be precisely defined. Artistic imagery does not conform to scientific precision and a certain margin of indetermination must be maintained. It is therefore possible for a critic to use the term broadly, but one is well advised to distinguish between "ordinary" destruction, which can be followed by reconstruction, and the irreversible physical process of entropic disintegration. In other words, not all literature of despair and catastrophe is necessarily entropic.

The term's real significance for contemporary literature lies in its ability to bring together and explain physical and social phenomena which at first may seem to have very little in common. While the concept cannot explain all aspects of our reality, it brings together enough seemingly unrelated structures to make it a meaningful element of the cognitive process. Their common denominator in literature is the vision of man faced with forces that keep destroying his world and himself, while he can do nothing to stop or reverse the process. What makes the process even more ineluctable is that the destruction is totally "impersonal," and the victim is faced with forces which destroy him not because of what he is but because of where he happens to be. Consequently, the only way he can survive is to tear away from his environment. It is an action equivalent to breaking out of a closed system in physics, and just as difficult.

Whenever a term is transferred from the sciences to the arts and humanities, it stands to lose some of its clarity and sharpness. Instead of attempting the impossible task of restoring its purity of meaning, we may consider the compensations, which in this case would consist of the concept's ability to inspire and explain works of art. It seems that entropy fulfills this role very successfully, particularly in contemporary American fiction. Whether our world will actually end in a whimper is a different question altogether, but enough writers share this view to consider such a possibility seriously—and not only in relation to their own works.

Entropy has not replaced apocalypse as a metaphor for the destruction of the world. The two concepts co-exist in contemporary fiction, expressing the conviction that people have no ultimate power over the universe. It can be brought to an end by forces—divine or natural—that man cannot control. The resulting sense of impending destruction has dominated American consciousness, and literature, for centuries. It has, however, changed over the years, not only because the concept of apocalypse has partly lost its regenerative promise, but also because the idea of entropic death can offer nothing but the fear of destruction.

Apocalypse and entropy originated in different conceptual frameworks, and they have different overall meanings. Yet as literary metaphors they have a similar effect: of projecting a sense of loss and danger. The continuing presence of such visions in American literature can thus provide a significant insight into the process of shaping the American mind.

NOTES

1. William Gaddis, *JR*, p. 20. Subsequent references in parentheses are to this edition.

2. Max Planck, *Eight Lectures on Theoretical Physics*, p. 50.

3. Susan Sontag, *Death Kit*, p. 2. Subsequent references in parentheses are to this edition.

4. The experience of passing through a tunnel was repeatedly cited by survivors of biological death (cf., for instance, Raymond A. Moody, *Life After Life*). Susan Sontag's description of Diddy's tunnel with its time and space perturbations bears a distinct resemblance to the "death tunnel."

5. John Updike, *Rabbit, Run*, p. 28. Subsequent references in parentheses are to this edition.

6. John Updike, *Rabbit Redux*, p. 388.

7. John Updike, *Couples*, p. 30. Subsequent references in parentheses are to this edition.

BIBLIOGRAPHY

PRIMARY SOURCES

Adams, Henry. *The Education of Henry Adams*. New York: Modern Library, 1946.

Bradford, William. *Of Plymouth Plantation 1620-1647*. Edited by Samuel Eliot Morison. New York: Modern Library, 1967.

Clemens, Samuel Langhorne. *The Complete Essays of Mark Twain*. Edited by Charles Neider. Garden City, N.Y.: Doubleday and Co., 1963.

———. *A Connecticut Yankee in King Arthur's Court*. Reprint of the 1889 ed. Ann Arbor: University Microfilms, 1966.

———. *Mark Twain's Mysterious Stranger Manuscripts*. Edited by William M. Gibson. Berkeley: University of California Press, 1969.

———. "Reflections on Religion," edited by Charles Neider. *Hudson Review*, 16 (Autumn 1963): 329-52.

Coover, Robert. *The Origin of the Brunists*. New York: G. P. Putnam's Sons, 1966.

———. *The Public Burning*. New York: Viking Press, 1977.

———. *The Universal Baseball Association, Inc., J. Henry Waugh, Prop.* New York: Random House, 1968.

Cotton, John. *The Churches Resurrection*. London: Printed by R. O. and G. D. for Henry Overton, 1642.

———. *An Exposition upon the Thirteenth Chapter of the Revelation*. London: Printed by M. S. for Livewel Chapman, 1655.

———. *Gods Promise to His Plantation*. London: John Bellamy, 1630.

————. *The Powring out of the Seven Vials: or an Exposition, of the 16 Chapter of the Revelation, with an Application of It to Our Times*. London: Printed for R. S., 1642.

Edwards, Jonathan. *Apocalyptic Writings*. Edited by Stephen J. Stein. New Haven: Yale University Press, 1977.

————. *The Great Awakening*. Edited by C. C. Goen. New Haven: Yale University Press, 1972.

————. *Sermons on Various Important Subjects*. Boston: Printed in Edinburgh; reprinted for M. Gray, 1785.

————. *Twenty Sermons on Different Subjects*. Carlisle: Printed by George Kline, 1803.

————. *The Works of President Edwards, in Ten Volumes*. New York: G. & C. & H. Carvill, 1830.

Ellison, Ralph. *Invisible Man*. New York: Random House, 1952.

Gaddis, William. *JR*. New York: Knopf, 1975.

Johnson, Edward. *Wonder-Working Providence of Sion's Saviour in New England*. Andover: W. F. Draper, 1867.

Mather, Cotton. *Magnalia Christi Americana*. Edited by Kenneth B. Murdock. Cambridge, Mass.: Belknap Press of Harvard University Press, 1977.

Mather, Increase. *The Necessity of Reformation*. Boston: Printed by John Foster, 1679.

Melville, Herman. *Bartleby the Scrivener*, in *Five Tales*. New York: Dodd, Mead and Co., 1967.

————. *Moby Dick*. New York: Charles Scribner's Sons, 1899.

Morgan, Joseph. *The History of the Kingdom of Basaruah* and *Three Unpublished Letters*. Edited by Richard Schlatter. Cambridge, Mass.: Harvard University Press, 1946.

Pynchon, Thomas. *The Crying of Lot 49*. Philadelphia: J. B. Lippincott, 1966.

————. "Entropy," *Kenyon Review*, 22 (Spring 1960): 277-92.

————. *Gravity's Rainbow*. New York: Viking Press, 1973.

————. *V*. Philadelphia: J.B. Lippincott, 1963.

Sontag, Susan. *Death Kit*. New York: Farrar, Straus and Giroux, 1967.

Updike, John. *Couples*. New York: Knopf, 1968.

————. *Marry Me*. New York: Knopf, 1976.

————. *Rabbit Redux*. New York: Knopf, 1971.

————. *Rabbit, Run*. New York: Knopf, 1960.

West, Nathanael. *A Cool Million* and *The Dream Life of Balso Snell*. New York: Avon Books, 1973.

————. *The Day of the Locust*. New York: Random House, 1939.

————. *Miss Lonelyhearts*. New York: Liveright, 1933.

Wigglesworth, Michael. *The Day of Doom*. 1st ed. 1662. New York: American News Co., 1867.

SECONDARY SOURCES

Aaron, Daniel. "Waiting for the Apocalypse," *Hudson Review*, 3 (Winter 1951): 634-36.

Abernathy, Peter. "Entropy in Pynchon's *The Crying of Lot 49*," *Critique*, 14 (1972): 18-33.

Adams, Henry. *The Degradation of the Democratic Dogma*. Reprint of the 1919 ed. New York: Harper Torchbooks, 1969.

Aldridge, John. *After the Lost Generation*. Freeport, N.Y.: Books for Libraries Press, 1971.

Alter, Robert. "The Apocalyptic Temper," *Commentary*, 41 (June 1966): 61-66.

Altizer, Thomas J.J. "Imagination and Apocalypse," *Soundings*, 53 (Winter 1970): 398-412.

Anderson, Kenneth. "The Ending of Mark Twain's *A Connecticut Yankee in King Arthur's Court*," *Mark Twain Journal*, 14 (Summer 1969): 21.

Angrist, Stanley W., and Loren G. Hepler. *Order and Chaos: Laws of Energy and Entropy*. New York: Basic Books, 1967.

Arac, Jonathan. *Commissioned Spirits*. New Brunswick, N.J.: Rutgers University Press, 1979.

Arnheim, Rudolf. *Entropy and Art: An Essay on Disorder and Order*. Berkeley: University of California Press, 1971.

Arvin, Newton. *Herman Melville*. New York: William Sloan Associates, 1950.

Babcock, C. Merton. "Mark Twain's Religious Creed," *Southern California Quarterly*, 48 (June 1966): 169-74.

Baldwin, Kenneth H., and David K. Kirby, eds. *Individual and Community*. Durham, N.C.: Duke University Press, 1975.

Banta, Martha. "American Apocalypses: Excrement and Ennui," *Studies in the Literary Imagination*, 7 (Spring 1974): 1-30.

Baumbach, Jonathan. *The Landscape of Nightmare*. New York: New York University Press, 1965.

Beardslee, William A. *America and the Future of Theology*. Philadelphia: Westminster Press, 1967.

Beebe, Maurice, ed. *Literary Symbolism*. San Francisco: Wadsworth Publishing Co., 1960.

Bellamy, Joe David, ed. *Apocalypse: Dominant Contemporary Forms*. Philadelphia: J. B. Lippincott, 1972.

Bellman, Samuel Irving. "The Apocalypse in Literature," *Costerus*, 7 (1973): 13-25.

Bercovitch, Sacvan. *The American Jeremiad*. Madison: University of Wisconsin Press, 1978.

————. "The Historiography of Johnson's *Wonder-Working Providence,*" *Essex Institute Historical Collections,* 104 (April 1968): 138-61.

————. "Horologicals to Chronometricals: The Rhetoric of the Jeremiad," *Literary Monographs,* vol. 3. Edited by Eric Rothstein. Madison: University of Wisconsin Press, 1970.

————. "Typology in Puritan New England: The Williams-Cotton Controversy Reassessed," *American Quarterly,* 19, no. 2 (Summer 1967): 166-91.

Berryman, Charles. *From Wilderness to Wasteland: The Trial of the Puritan God in the American Imagination.* Port Washington, N.Y.: Kennikat Press, 1979.

Bischoff, Joan. "With Manic Laughter: The Secular Apocalypse in American Novels of the 1960's." Ph.D. dissertation, Lehigh University, 1975.

Black World, 20 (Dec. 1970) (special issue on Ralph Ellison).

Blues, Thomas. *Mark Twain and the Community.* Lexington: University Press of Kentucky, 1970.

Boklund, Gunnar. "Time Must Have a Stop: Apocalyptic Thought and Expression in the Twentieth Century," *University of Denver Quarterly,* 2 (Summer 1967): 69-98.

Bowman, John S. "The Agony and the Entropy," *Harvard Magazine,* 81 (Nov./Dec. 1978): 14-16.

Bradbury, Malcolm. *Possibilities: Essays on the State of the Novel.* London: Oxford University Press, 1973.

Brillouin, Leon. *Science and Information Theory.* New York: Academic Press, 1956.

Brodtkorb, Paul, Jr. *Ishmael's White World: A Phenomenological Reading of "Moby Dick."* New Haven: Yale University Press, 1965.

Brouer, Reuben A., ed. *Twentieth Century Literature in Retrospect.* Cambridge, Mass.: Harvard University Press, 1971.

Buber, Martin. *Paths in Utopia.* Translated by R.F.C. Hull. New York: Macmillan Company, 1950.

————. *Pointing the Way.* Translated by Maurice Friedman. London: Routledge and Kegan Paul, 1957.

Budd, Louis J., Edwin H. Cady, and Carl L. Anderson, eds. *Toward a New American Literary History.* Durham, N.C.: Duke University Press, 1980.

Callahan, John F. "Chaos, Complexity and Possibility: The Historical Frequencies of Ralph Waldo Ellison," *Black American Literature Forum,* 11 (Winter 1977): 130-38.

Campbell, Will D., and James Y. Holloway, eds. *The Failure and the Hope: Essays of Southern Churchmen.* Grand Rapids, Mich.: William B. Eerdmans Publishing Co., 1972.

Case, Shirley Jackson. *The Millennial Hope: A Phase of War-Time Thinking.* Chicago: University of Chicago Press, 1918.

Chander, Jagdish, and Narindar Pradhan. *Studies in American Literature.* Delhi: Oxford University Press, 1976.

Charles, R. H. *Eschatology: The Doctorine of Future Life in Israel, Judaism and Christianity.* New York: Schocken Books, 1963.

Clark, Neill Wilson, III. "The Metaphor of Apocalypse in the Fiction of Nathanael West." Ph.D. dissertation, Emory University, 1976.

Clipper, Lawrence J. "Folkloric and Mythic Elements in *Invisible Man,*" *College Language Association Journal,* 13 (March 1970): 229-41.

Coad, Oral Sumner. "The Gothic Element in American Literature," *Journal of English and Germanic Philology,* 24 (January 1925): 72-93.

Cohn, Norman Rufus Colin. *The Pursuit of the Millennium.* Fairlawn, N.J.: Essential Books, 1957.

Collins, Angus Paul. "Three Apocalyptic Novels." Ph.D. dissertation, Indiana University, 1976.

Combs, Barbara. "*The Confidence Man* as Apocalyptic Vision." Ph.D. dissertation, Ohio State University, 1972.

Cook, Dayton Grover. "The Apocalyptic Novel: *Moby Dick* and *Doktor Faustus.*" Ph.D. dissertation, University of Colorado, 1974.

Cox, James M. "*A Connecticut Yankee in King Arthur's Court*: The Machinery of Self Preservation," *Yale Review,* 50 (Autumn 1960): 89-102.

————. *Mark Twain: The Fate of Humor.* Princeton: Princeton University Press, 1966.

Creeger, George. "Color Symbolism in the Works of Herman Melville 1846-1852." Ph.D. dissertation, Yale University, 1952.

————. "The Symbolism of Whiteness in Melville's Prose Fiction," *Jahrbuch für Amerikastudien,* Band 5, Heidelberg: Carl Winter Universitätsverlag, 1960.

Cross, Barbara M. "Apocalypse as Comedy in *As I Lay Dying,*" *Texas Studies in Literature and Language,* 3 (Summer 1961): 251-58.

Dahl, Curtis. "The American School of Catastrophe," *American Quarterly,* 11 (Fall 1959): 380-90.

Davidson, Frank. "*Bartleby*: A Few Observations," *Emerson Society Quarterly,* 27 (1962): 25-32.

Davis, Thomas M., and Virginia L. Davis. "Edward Taylor on the Day of Judgment," *American Literature,* 43 (1972): 525-47.

Dillard, R. H. W. "The Wisdom of the Beast: The Fictions of Robert Coover," *The Hollins Critic,* 7 (April 1970): 1-11.

Dolloff, Norman. *Heat Death and the Phoenix: Entropy, Order and the Future of Man.* Hicksville, N.Y.: Exposition Press, 1975.

Eliade, Mircea. *Cosmos and History: The Myth of the Eternal Return.* Translated by Willard R. Trask. New York: Harper and Brothers, 1959.

————. *Myth and Reality.* Translated by Willard R. Trask. New York: Harper and Row, 1963.

Ellison, Ralph. *Shadow and Act.* New York: Random House, 1964.

Elsbree, Oliver Wendell. *The Rise of the Missionary Spirit in America 1790-1815.* Philadelphia: Porcupine Press, 1980.

Ensor, Allison. *Mark Twain and the Bible*. Lexington: University of Kentucky Press, 1969.

Feidelson, Charles, Jr. *Symbolism and American Literature*. Chicago: University of Chicago Press, 1953.

Feuillet, André. *The Apocalypse*. Translated by Thomas E. Crane. Staten Island, N.Y.: Alba House, 1965.

Fiedler, Leslie A. *Love and Death in the American Novel*. New York: Criterion Books, 1960.

————. *Waiting for the End*. New York: Stein and Day, 1964.

Franklin, H. Bruce. *The Wake of the Gods: Melville's Mythology*. Stanford: Stanford University Press, 1963.

French, Warren, ed. *The Forties: Fiction, Poetry, Drama*. Deland, Fla.: Everett/ Edwards, 1969.

Friedman, Alan J., and Manfred Pütz." Science as Metaphor: Thomas Pynchon and *Gravity's Rainbow*," *Contemporary Literature*, 15 (Summer 1974): 345-59.

Froom, LeRoy Edwin. *The Prophetic Faith of Our Fathers: The Historical Development of Prophetic Interpretations*. 4 vols. Washington, D.C.: Review and Herald, 1946-1954.

Frye, Northrop. *Anatomy of Criticism: Four Essays*. Princeton: Princeton University Press, 1957.

Fussell, Edwin. "Hawthorne, James and 'The Common Doom,' " *American Quarterly*, 10 (Winter 1958): 438-53.

Galloway, David D. *The Absurd Hero in American Fiction*. Austin: University of Texas Press, 1970.

Gaustad, Edwin Scott. *The Great Awakening in New England*. New York: Harper and Brothers, 1957.

Gay, Peter. *A Loss of Mastery: Puritan Historians in Colonial America*. Berkeley: University of California Press, 1966.

Gayle, Addison, Jr., ed. *The Black Aesthetic*. Garden City, N.Y.: Anchor Books, 1972.

Geiger, Don. "Demonism in *Moby Dick*: A Study of Twelve Chapters," *Perspective*, 6 (Spring 1953): 111-24.

Gerlach, John C. "The Kingdom of God and Nineteenth Century American Fiction." Ph.D. dissertation, Arizona State University, 1969.

Gervais, Ronald J. "*The Mysterious Stranger:* The Fall as Salvation," *Pacific Coast Philology*, 5 (April 1970): 24-33.

Gibson, Donald B., ed. *Five Black Writers*. New York: New York University Press, 1970.

Gillespie, Gerald. "New Apocalypse for Old: Kermode's Theory of Modernism," *Boundary 2*, 3 (Winter 1975): 307-23.

Gilman, Richard. *The Confusion of Realms*. New York: Random House, 1969.

Gilmore, Michael T. "Melville's Apocalypse: American Millennialism and *Moby Dick*," *Emerson Society Quarterly*, 21 (1975): 154-61.

————. *The Middle Way: Puritanism and Ideology in American Romantic Fiction*. New Brunswick, N.J.: Rutgers University Press, 1977.

Gilsdorf, Jay Bourne. "The Puritan Apocalypse: New England Eschatology in the Seventeenth Century." Ph.D. dissertation, Yale University, 1964.

Godbey, Allen H. *The Lost Tribes: A Myth*. New York: Ktav Publishing House, 1974.

Goodheart, Eugene. "The New Apocalypse," *The Nation*, 201 (1965): 207-11.

Gottesman, Ronald, ed. *The Merrill Studies in "Invisible Man."* Columbus, Ohio: Charles E. Merrill Publishing Co., 1971.

Gray, Valerie Bonita. *"Invisible Man's" Literary Heritage: "Benito Cereno" and "Moby Dick."* Amsterdam: Rodopi, 1978.

Green, Jesse D. "Diabolism, Pessimism, and Democracy: Notes on Melville and Conrad," *Modern Fiction Studies*, 8 (Autumn 1962): 287-305.

Greenberg, Alvin David. "The Novel of Disintegration." Ph.D. dissertation, University of Washington, 1964.

Haller, William. *The Rise of Puritanism*. New York: Harper and Brothers, 1938.

Harnsberger, Caroline T. *Mark Twain's Views of Religion*. Evanston, Ill.: Schori Press, 1961.

Harrington, Wilfrid J. *The Apocalypse of St. John: A Commentary*. London: Geoffrey Chapman, 1969.

Harrison, J.F.C. *The Second Coming: Popular Millennialism*. New Brunswick, N.J.: Rutgers University Press, 1979.

Hausdorff, Don. "Thomas Pynchon's Multiple Absurdities," *Wisconsin Studies in Contemporary Literature*, 7 (Autumn 1966): 258-69.

Hays, John Q. "Mark Twain's Rebellion Against God: Origins," *Southwestern American Literature*, 3 (1973): 27-38.

Heimert, Alan. *Religion and the American Mind*. Cambridge, Mass.: Harvard University Press, 1966.

Hemenway, Robert, ed. *The Black Novelist*. Columbus, Ohio: Charles E. Merrill Publishing Co., 1970.

Henderson, Harry B., III. *Visions of the Past: The Historical Imagination in American Fiction*. New York: Oxford University Press, 1974.

Herbert, T. Walker, Jr. *"Moby Dick" and Calvinism*. New Brunswick, N.J.: Rutgers University Press, 1977.

Hertzel, Leo J. "What's Wrong with the Christians." *Critique*, 11 (1969): 11-22.

Hill, Hamlin. *Mark Twain: God's Fool*. New York: Harper and Row, 1973.

Hilton, Earl. "Mark Twain's Theory of History," *Michigan Academy of Science, Arts and Letters*, 37 (1951): 445-53.

Hirsch, David. "The Pit and the Apocalypse," *Sewanee Review*, 77 (1968): 632-52.

Hochfield, George. *Henry Adams*. New York: Barnes and Noble, 1962.

Hoeltje, Hubert. "Hawthorne, Melville, and 'Blackness,' " *American Literature*, 37 (March 1965): 41-51.

Howe, Irving. "James Baldwin: At Ease in Apocalypse," review of *Tell Me How Long the Train's Been Gone*. *Harper's*, 237 (September 1968): 92-100.

———. *A World More Attractive*. New York: Horizon Press, 1963.

Husni, Khalil. "The Whiteness of the Whale: A Survey of Interpretations, 1851-1970," *College Language Association Journal*, 20 (Dec. 1976): 210-21.

Hyman, Stanley Edgar. *The Promised End*. Cleveland: World Publishing Co., 1963.

Jaher, Frederic Cople. *Doubters and Dissenters: Cataclysmic Thought in America 1885-1918*. New York: Free Press of Glencoe, 1964.

Kappel, Lawrence. "Psychic Geography in *Gravity's Rainbow*," *Contemporary Literature*, 21 (1980): 225-51.

Kasson, John. *Civilizing the Machine*. New York: Penguin, 1976.

Kermode, Frank. *Continuities*. New York: Random House, 1968.

———. "The New Apocalyptists," *Partisan Review*, 33 (Summer 1966): 339-61.

———. *The Sense of an Ending*. New York: Oxford University Press, 1967.

Ketterer, David. *New Worlds for Old: The Apocalyptic Imagination*. Garden City, N.Y.: Anchor Press, 1974.

Killinger, John. "Death of God in American Literature," *Southern Humanities Review*, 2 (Spring 1968): 149-72.

Klein, Marcus. *After Alienation*. Freeport, N.Y.: Books for Libraries Press, 1964.

Knickerbocker, Conrad. "William Burroughs. An Interview," *Paris Review*, 35 (Fall 1965): 13-50.

Koch, Klaus. *The Rediscovery of Apocalyptic*. Translated by Margaret Kohl. London: SCM Press, 1972.

Kostelanetz, Richard, ed. *On Contemporary Literature*. Freeport, N.Y.: Books for Libraries Press, 1971.

Lasch, Christopher. "Mumford and the Myth of the Machine," *Salmagundi*, 49 (Summer 1980): 4-28.

Lee, A. Robert, ed. *Black Fiction: New Studies in the Afro-American Novel Since 1945*. New York: Harper and Row, 1980.

Leland, John P. "Pynchon's Linguistic Demon: *The Crying of Lot 49*," *Critique*, 16 (1974): 45-53.

Lévi-Strauss, Claude. *Tristes Tropiques*. Translated by John and Doreen Weightman. London: Cape, 1973.

Levin, Harry. *The Power of Blackness*. New York: Knopf, 1967.

Levine, George, and David Leverenz, eds. *Mindful Pleasures*. Boston: Little, Brown and Co., 1976.

Lewis, C. S. *The World's Last Night*. New York: Harcourt, Brace and Co., 1960.

Lewis, R.W.B. *The American Adam*. Chicago: University of Chicago Press, 1955.

———. *Trials of the Word*. New Haven: Yale University Press, 1965.

L'Heureux, John. "On The Eighth Day: The Death of God in Contemporary American Literature," *Critic*, 24 (June/July 1966): 46-55.

Lodge, David. *The Novelist at the Crossroads*. Ithaca, N.Y.: Cornell University Press, 1971.

Luccock, Halford E. *Contemporary American Literature and Religion*. Chicago: Willett, Clark and Co., 1934.

Lyons, Thomas R., and Allan D. Franklin. "Thomas Pynchon's 'Classic' Presentation of the Second Law of Thermodynamics," *Bulletin of the Rocky Mountain Modern Language Association*, 27 (1972): 195-204.

McConnell, Frank D. *Four Postwar American Novelists*. Chicago: University of Chicago Press, 1977.

McCormick, John. *Catastrophe and Imagination: An Interpretation of the Recent English and American Novel*. London: Longmans, 1957.

McGinn, Bernard. *Visions of the End: Apocalyptic Traditions in the Middle Ages*. New York: Columbia University Press, 1979.

Maclear, J. F. "New England and the Fifth Monarchy," *William and Mary Quarterly*, 3rd series, 32 (April 1975): 223-60.

Madden, David, ed. *American Dreams, American Nightmares*. Carbondale: Southern Illinois University Press, 1970.

———. *Rediscoveries*. New York: Crown Publishers, 1971.

Magaw, Malcomb. "Apocalyptic Imagery in Melville's 'The Apple Tree Table,' " *Midwest Quarterly*, 8 (1967): 357-69.

Mangel, Anne. "Maxwell's Demon, Entropy, Information: *The Crying of Lot 49*," *TriQuarterly*, 20 (Winter 1971): 194-208.

Mason, Ronald. *The Spirit Above the Dust: A Study of Herman Melville*. Mamaroneck, N.Y.: Paul P. Appel, 1972.

Matthiessen, F. O. *American Renaissance: Art and Expression in the Age of Emerson and Whitman*. London: Oxford University Press, 1941.

May, John R. *Toward a New Earth: Apocalypse in the American Novel*. Notre Dame, Ind.: University of Notre Dame Press, 1972.

Mendelson, Edward, ed. *Pynchon: A Collection of Critical Essays*. Englewood Cliffs, N.J.: Prentice-Hall, 1978.

Middlekauff, Robert. *The Mathers: Three Generations of Puritan Intellectuals*. New York: Oxford University Press, 1971.

Miller, Joseph Hillis. *Poets of Reality: Six Twentieth Century Writers*. Cambridge, Mass.: Belknap Press of Harvard University Press, 1965.

Miller, Perry. "The End of the World," *William and Mary Quarterly*, 3rd series, 8 (April 1951): 171-91.

———. *Errand into the Wilderness*. Cambridge, Mass.: Belknap Press of Harvard University Press, 1956.

———. *The Life of the Mind in America: From the Revolution to the Civil War*. London: Victor Gollancz, 1966.

———. *The New England Mind: From Colony to Province*. Cambridge, Mass.: Harvard University Press, 1967.

———. *The New England Mind: The Seventeenth Century*. Cambridge, Mass.: Harvard University Press, 1967.

Moles, Abraham. *Information Theory and Esthetic Perception*. Translated by Joel E. Cohen. Urbana: University of Illinois Press, 1968.

Moody, Raymond A. *Life After Life*. Harrisburg, Pa.: Stackpole Books, 1976.

Mooney, Harry J., Jr., and Thomas F. Staley, eds. *The Shapeless God*. Pittsburgh: University of Pittsburgh Press, 1968.

Morgan, Speer. *"Gravity's Rainbow*: What's the Big Idea?" *Modern Fiction Studies*, 23 (Summer 1977): 199-216.

Morris, Leon. *Apocalyptic*. Grand Rapids, Mich.: William B. Eerdmans Publishing Co., 1972.

Moses, W. R. "The Pattern of Evil in *Adventures of Huckleberry Finn*," *Georgia Review*, 13 (Summer 1959): 161-66.

Murdock, Kenneth. Introduction. *Day of Doom*, by Michael Wigglesworth. New York: Spiral Press, 1929.

Newlin, Claude M. *Philosophy and Religion in Colonial America*. New York: Philosophical Library, 1962.

Nicolson, Marjorie Hope. *Mountain Gloom and Mountain Glory: The Development of the Aesthetics of the Infinite*. Ithaca, N.Y.: Cornell University Press, 1959.

Niebuhr, H. Richard. *The Kingdom of God in America*. Chicago: Willett, Clark and Co., 1937.

O'Brien, Conor Cruise. "Purely American," *Harper's*, 260 (April 1980): 32-34.

Parsons, Coleman O. "The Devil and Samuel Clemens," *Virginia Quarterly Review*, 23 (Autumn 1947): 582-606.

Patteson, Richard. "What Stencil Knew: Structure and Certitude in Pynchon's *V.*," *Critique*, 16 (1974): 30-44.

Pearce, Richard. " 'Pylon,' 'Awake and Sing!' and the Apocalyptic Imagination of the 30's," *Criticism*, 13 (Spring 1971): 131-41.

Planck, Max. *Eight Lectures on Theoretical Physics*. Translated by A. P. Wills, New York: Columbia University Press, 1915.

Plater, William M. *The Grim Phoenix*. Bloomington: Indiana University Press, 1978.

Plumstead, A. W. "Puritanism and Nineteenth Century American Literature," *Queen's Quarterly*, 70 (Summer 1963): 209-22.

Poirier, Richard. *The Performing Self*. New York: Oxford University Press, 1971.

Porush, David. "Apocalypse of the 60's: A Study of the Morphology of a Literary Genre." Ph.D. dissertation, State University of New York at Buffalo, 1977.

Rees, Robert A. "Mark Twain and the Bible: Characters Who Use the Bible and Biblical Characters." Ph.D. dissertation, University of Wisconsin, 1966.

Regan, Robert. *Unpromising Heroes*. Berkeley: University of California Press, 1966.

Reimer, Earl A. "Mark Twain and the Bible: An Introductory Study." Ph.D. dissertation, Michigan State University, 1970.

Ricoeur, Paul. *The Symbolism of Evil*. Translated by Emerson Buchanan. New York: Harper and Row, 1967.

Rodway, Allan. *The Truths of Fiction*. New York: Schocken Books, 1971.

Rosenmeier, Jesper. "The Teacher and the Witness," *William and Mary Quarterly*, 3rd series, 25 (July 1968): 408-31.

Roth, Richard. "*Fin-de-siècle* and *fin-du-monde*: The Apocalypse of American Power in *A Connecticut Yankee* and *The Education of Henry Adams*" (paper delivered at the First International Symposium on American Literature, University of Warsaw, 1978).

Rovit, Earl. "On the Contemporary Apocalyptic Imagination," *American Scholar*, 37 (Summer 1968): 453-68.

Russell, D. S. *Apocalyptic: Ancient and Modern*. Philadelphia: Fortress Press, 1978.

Salomon, Roger B. *Twain and the Image of History*. New Haven: Yale University Press, 1961.

Schall, James V. "The Apocalypse as a Secular Enterprise," *Scottish Journal of Theology*, 29 (1976): 357-73.

Scheick, William J. "The Grand Design: Jonathan Edwards' *History of the Work of Redemption*," *Eighteenth-Century Studies*, 8 (Spring 1975): 300-314.

Scherer, Olga. "Une Allégorie Apocalyptique du 'Postromantisme': Melville et Norwid," *Revue de Litterature Comparée*, 50 (Jan.-June, 1976): 168-83.

Schmithals, Walter. *The Apocalyptic Movement*. Translated by John E. Steely. Nashville: Abingdon Press, 1975.

Schmitz, Neil. "Describing the Demon: The Appeal of Thomas Pynchon," *Partisan Review*, 42 (1975): 112-25.

Schulz, Max F. *Black Humor Fiction of the Sixties*. Athens, Ohio: Ohio University Press, 1973.

Scott, Nathan A., Jr. " 'New Heav'ns, New Earth': The Landscape of Contemporary Apocalypse," *Journal of Religion*, 53 (Jan. 1973): 1-35.

―――. *The Tragic Vision and the Christian Faith*. New York: Association Press, 1957.

————, ed. *Adversity and Grace*. Chicago: University of Chicago Press, 1968.

Scott, Robert Ian. "A Sense of Loss: Entropy vs. Ecology in *The Great Gatsby*," *Queen's Quarterly*, 82 (Winter 1975): 559-71.

Sedgwick, William Ellery. *Herman Melville: The Tragedy of Mind*. Cambridge, Mass.: Harvard University Press, 1944.

Seltzer, Alvin J. *Chaos in the Novel, the Novel in Chaos*. New York: Schocken Books, 1974.

Simmon, Scott. "*Gravity's Rainbow* Described," *Critique*, 16 (1974): 54-67.

Slade, Joseph W. *Thomas Pynchon*. New York: Warner Paperback Library, 1974.

Smith, David E. "Millenarian Scholarship in America," *American Quarterly*, 17 (Fall 1965): 535-49.

Smith, Samuela Dave Davidson. "Apocalyptic Symbolism in the Argentine Novel." Ph.D. dissertation, University of Kentucky, 1976.

Smith, Timothy L. *Revivalism and Social Reform in Mid-Nineteenth-Century America*. New York: Abingdon Press, 1957.

Snell, George. *The Shapers of American Fiction*. New York: E. P. Dutton and Co., 1947.

Spengeman, William C. *Mark Twain and the Backwoods Angel*. Kent, Ohio: Kent State University Press, 1966.

Springer, Norman. "*Bartleby* and the Terror of Limitation," *Publications of the Modern Language Association of America*, 80 (September 1965): 410-18.

Stewart, Randall. *American Literature and Christian Doctrine*. Baton Rouge: Louisiana State University Press, 1958.

Stone, Edward. *Voices of Despair*. Athens: Ohio University Press, 1966.

Stovall, Floyd, ed. *Eight American Authors*. New York: W. W. Norton and Co., 1971.

Sypher, Wylie. *Loss of the Self in Modern Literature and Art*. New York: Random House, 1962.

Tanner, Tony. *City of Words*. New York: Harper and Row, 1971.

————. "The Lost America: The Despair of Henry Adams and Mark Twain," *Modern Age*, 5 (Summer 1961): 299-310.

Thompson, Lawrence. *Melville's Quarrel with God*. Princeton: Princeton University Press, 1952.

Thrupp, Sylvia L. *Millennial Dreams in Action: Studies in Revolutionary Religious Movements*. New York: Schocken Books, 1970.

Trefz, Edward K. "The Puritans' View of History," *Boston Public Library Quarterly*, 9 (July 1957): 115-36.

Tuckey, John S., ed. *Mark Twain's "The Mysterious Stranger" and the Critics*. Belmont, Calif.: Wadsworth Publishing Co., 1968.

Tuveson, Ernest Lee. *Millennium and Utopia*. Berkeley: University of California Press, 1949.

————. *Redeemer Nation*. Chicago: University of Chicago Press, 1968.

Ujházy, Maria. "Melville's Use of Mythology," *Acta Litteraria Academiae Scientiarum Hungaricae*, 20 (1978): 53-63.

Waggoner, Hyatt Howe. "Science in the Thought of Mark Twain," *American Literature*, 8 (January 1937): 357-70.

Watters, R. E. "Melville's Metaphysics of Evil," *University of Toronto Quarterly*, 9 (January 1940): 170-82.

Weinstein, Arnold L. *Vision and Response in Modern Fiction*. Ithaca, N.Y.: Cornell University Press, 1974.

Werge, Thomas. "Mark Twain and the Fall of Adam," *Mark Twain Journal*, 15 (Summer 1970): 5-13.

West, Victor Royce. *Folklore in the Works of Mark Twain*. Reprint of the 1930 ed. Folcraft, Pa.: Folcraft Library Editions, 1974.

Wiener, Norbert. *The Human Use of Human Beings*. Boston: Houghton Mifflin, 1954.

Wink, Walter. "Apocalypse in Our Time," *Katallagete*, 3 (Fall 1970): 13-18.

Wolfley, Lawrence C. "Repression Rainbow: The Presence of Norman O. Brown in Pynchon's Big Novel," *Publications of the Modern Language Association of America*, 92 (October 1977): 873-89.

Wright, Nathalia. *Melville's Use of the Bible*. New York: Octagon Press, 1969.

Young, James Dean. "The Enigma Variations of Thomas Pynchon," *Critique*, 10 (1968): 69-77.

Zavarzadeh, Mas'ud. "The Apocalyptic Fact and the Eclipse of Fiction in Recent American Prose Narratives," *American Studies*, 9 (1975): 69-83.

Ziff, Larzer. *The Career of John Cotton: Puritanism and the American Experience*. Princeton: Princeton University Press, 1962.

INDEX

About the Author

ZBIGNIEW LEWICKI is Chairman of the American Literature Department at the University of Warsaw, Poland. His previous books are *Time in the Stream-of-Consciousness Novel* and two anthologies: *Contemporary American Short Fiction* and *Contemporary American Literary Criticism*. He has also contributed to numerous Polish and American journals.